Timeless Awakening

Timeless Awakening

A Spiritual Path for Aligning with Your Divine Self

Shariq Mahbub

2011

Dedication

I dedicate this book to HMP, who has been a bastion of support for anchoring these words of wisdom into this Earth plane.

Thank you, dearest one, for your support, love, patience, endurance and inherent sweetness, that is, indeed, the essence of life and creation.

Table of Contents

"Come forth into the light of things,
Let Nature be your teacher"
   - William Wordsworth, *The Tables Turned*

"And what if all of animated nature
Be but organic Harps diversely framed,
That tremble into thought, as o'er them sweeps
Plastic and vast, one intellectual breeze,
At once the Soul of each, and God of all?"
   - Samuel Taylor Coleridge, *The Aeolian Harp*

"I was
And I am
So shall I be to the end of time,
For I am without end."
   - Kahlil Gibran, *The Hymn of Man*

About the Author

Shariq Mahbub is a Spiritual teacher, author, clairvoyant, healer, medium and channel for the Ascended Masters, Archangels and other Galactic & Cosmic beings of light available to assist humanity at this exciting time of planetary ascension.

Please visit www.goldsunhealing.com for more information, including details about scheduling individual consultations.

Preface

It is with a humble heart and deep-felt gratitude for this moment and time of manifestation that I offer you this compendium of awakening words and energetics from Spirit, to guide us at this momentous time of a Shift in Consciousness.

One that is already promising to far exceed any of our conceptions of how life can change for the better, of how the love of who you are can consciously create the reality that you have always desired: full of fun, friends, laughter, abundance, travel, adventure and community.

This book mirrors my own awakening journey, as Spirit had me channel different portions of the book at different stages of my awakening process, so that, just as the energetics that came through helped me wake up, they, too, can work their magic on you.

The 99 inspirational pieces contained in this book are meant to "turn you on" in a multidimensional way. As such, although the book is linear, its magic and healing is not.

Please feel free to open any piece, a chapter that calls to you, for you, a vast consciousness playing this game of duality, which is now moving into higher frequencies of love and light, you know exactly what you need. So trust your guidance. This will indeed grow for you as you grow into vaster realms of consciousness.

And, just, as I now have grown from an investment banker who was quite unconscious to a conscious channel, healer, medium, clairvoyant and teacher in my own life and profession, you, too, will find your own individual journey into your magnificence.

And the process of learning and growing is infinite, and never ends, as I, myself, claim my adventure of growth and expansion every day.

The time is now to "wake up" and claim your birthright as a conscious Creator of this reality.

Thank you for reading this book. I leave you with a humble heart and deep-felt gratitude. May the energetics of this book take you on the next step of your divine journey home to the Golden Age of Light and Love.

Shariq Mahbub
New York
January 11th, 2011

Introduction

by Ra, Kuthumi, Mother Mary, Hathors & Archangel Gabriel on behalf of all the Spirit Collaborators

Welcome reader, to this moment in time when you have picked up this book to investigate the potentials for your future.

Perhaps you have been intrigued by the attention that the world is giving to the phenomenon of 2012. Perhaps you have been noticing that belief systems, whether about the banking and financial systems, about the role of minorities as world leaders, or even the importance about taking action to save and protect the environment, have all been changing.

Perhaps you are simply following the urgings of an inner voice within your head that urgently tells you: "It is now time to investigate who it is that you really are. It is now time to let go of the illusions of being small, of being separate from other humans, of going it alone and directionless in a world that cares not about you. It is time, at this time of the so-called end of times, but what is actually the start of a beautiful new age, to grow into the knowledge of who you really are, and ascend into a higher vibrational reality."

And so, whatever your inclination or objective, we welcome you, O Reader, to this book, to these pages of wisdom, coming from an invisible realm, that aim to allow you to begin to release programming from your culture, environment and ancestral DNA that tells you that your life is short, brutish and meaningless; that you only live once; that if you believe in life after death, it is a scary temple of judgment you will be brought to, where the chances of perdition, of being sent to hell are high, unless you buckle down to a religious path of a monotheistic, hierarchical religion; that Armageddon is at hand.

Instead, we choose to align you with a higher knowledge, one that pre-dates all of your cultures and religions, one that is ancient, infinite and always present. We choose to awaken in you an understanding of the wider expanse of your reality.

First, we ask you to consider that this world you live in, this Earth that you inhabit is like a game board for a game of duality that you all agreed to participate in, indeed, volunteered to participate in. The game board is a 3 dimensional holograph, and you, as a Spirit, as a being that is infinitely large and always existing, chose to enter into a human body, not just with the human body you inhabit today, but in many human bodies across many lifetimes, reincarnating again and again, creating **karma** across the karmic wheel of existence in this holograph called Earth.

Why would you choose to do this you ask? Isn't life difficult? Why would you choose a world of hunger, of anger, of poverty, of violence, of rage, of destruction, of intimidation, of repression? But it is also a world of opposites, is it not? You also experience in this world, the other set of extremes: a full and satisfied stomach, unconditional love for your child, riches, loving caresses, submissiveness, self-sacrifice, prostration and assertion. It is indeed a game of duality, one where you find yourself experiencing many emotions and circumstances, some pleasant, some wonderful, and many debilitating and awful.

Well, dear ones, we tell you that, as a Spiritual being, you have always been an adventurer, a creator, and you seek new experiences. In a sense, you could say that, as a part of Source, you left behind wider vistas of your expansive self to come to this third dimensional plane to understand yourself more clearly through contrast.

For, outside of this reality, outside of this holograph of duality, in the higher dimensional realities that you and your planet Earth are rapidly moving towards, all is love and light, fully aligned with the supreme knowledge that we all come from the same source, that we are connected, that in judging and hurting another, we are actually judging and hurting ourselves.

And so, you chose to incarnate on this planet, not once, but many times to experience duality and to store in your treasure trove of experiences that you call the **Akashic records**, the experiences of having experienced this game of karma, and gone through the cycle of 2012 towards the ascension of this planet and the game to a higher vibrational reality.

History and 2012

The Mayan prophecies talk about December 21ˢᵗ, 2012 as a date when our sun will align with the Galactic center of the Milky Way galaxy that we inhabit, in a cycle that takes 26,000 years, approximately, to complete. For the Mayans, they stopped computing their calendar on this date, leading modern interpreters to believe that this date presaged the end of the world, so to speak. And, certainly, this sense has been inflated by other mythologies, such as the book of Revelation in the Bible, the prophecies of Nostradamus and all the disaster movies and media hype about 2012 as the end of days.

We would like to first of all point out that 2012, and the events that surround the alignment of your sun with the Galactic Center cannot be limited to an exact date. It is a process, and it has already begun.

Not only is your sun aligning with the Galactic Center at this time, but other greater cycles of change are completing simultaneously, including the alignment of your Milky Way galaxy around the Central Sun of your Universe, providing for an evolutionary opportunity not only for your planet Earth, but for your entire galaxy.

And so, the actual date of December 21st is not as important as the fact that the process actually began commencing in 1987 during the Harmonic Convergence, and that the change has been a process that is in the final stages of unfolding. And, so do not wait till 2012. We urge and encourage you to explore who it is that you really are, to release the trappings of prior programming, and this book will show you how to start to do this, as the words and energy of the pieces of inspiration we share with you allow your bodies to release some of this programming, simply in the knowledge that we share with you, which will resonate with the truth already inside of you, your infinite truth, which will make your acquaintance once again, as you dust off the outer coverings of disguise with the energy of unconditional love, divine truth and wisdom.

Second, we would like to suggest that you release this notion that something bad, something limiting will happen to you in 2012. You have an opportunity now to very rapidly release the cloak of debilitation and of being small and meaningless that you have played in this 3rd dimensional game of duality. And you must take conscious steps to embrace change, for the change will be what you have dreamed of, and will exceed all such dreams.

For the Earth itself, as part of this galactic alignment, which takes place every 26,000 years or so, but is extra-special this time because of the alignment of the galaxy itself with the great Central Sun of your universe, is ascending. The vibrational reality is about to change from a 3rd dimensional holograph of duality to a 4th and 5th dimensional reality where lower vibrations of negativity, of violence, anger, rage, control, shame and general debilitation will have a very hard time maintaining any momentum.

And so, as spiritual beings in human bodies, you have an opportunity to ascend while alive, but to do this you must leave behind those prejudices and limitations and fears that tell you that you are less than you really are.

You must choose to embrace a wider notion of who it is that you are. And this book, in reading it, starts this process for you by unveiling your true self with its words.

By desiring to change, you start the process instantaneously. And what happens is that you begin to release pieces of energy from your energy body, which we will discuss in detail in the next section, that have cloaked you and allowed you to internalize vibrations of fear and hatred.

And sometimes you do not even know where your reactions are coming from, for you get angry and have an intense reaction to a person or event without knowing why. Well, part of this is the fact that you have energy patterns stored in your body from past lifetimes, and also cultural patterns in the ancestral DNA you inherited in your body that you must now release.

Think about each of the inspirational pieces in this book as a form of healing. Read each piece aloud first, and then again quietly, absorbing its message into your consciousness. The first time, the sounding of the words creates an opening, a movement of density that then allows your consciousness to integrate the wider range of meanings conveyed in our words as you open yourself to the change you are rapidly moving towards.

And we will also discuss in this book, how, as you begin leaving behind the limitations of who you are, you start a process of integrating aspects of your higher, multidimensional self into your changing human body. As a result, over time, as this ascension and New Age dawns, you will become much more intuitive, clairvoyant, telepathic and in touch with Spirit, getting messages directly from your personal angels and guides.

For, indeed, you are not alone, dear one. We are by your side constantly. We are holding your hands. We have got your back, so to speak. We are here to support your growth back into the wider expanse of who you really are.

And as you go through this process you will start seeing memories, while in meditation, of past lives. Initially these past lives will often be of unpleasant events, as your body begins to first of all release those pieces of energy that are really debilitating: the death scenes where you were punished for speaking your truth, where you learnt and stored in your frame the knowledge that it was better to hide who you were in order to survive in this game.

And then, you will start seeing images of earlier times, potentially, if they apply, of incarnations in ancient Atlantis and Lemuria, where, before **the "fall"** of consciousness into a 3rd dimensional reality, you were much more directly connected to the Spirit of all there is, and you understood that you were part of a community. And you had many gifts and talents back then that you will be reclaiming as you ascend in consciousness during this magnificent time of change.

We will talk more about Atlantis and Lemuria at a later date. For now we wish you to see an image of yourself as a note on one of the scales of a piano. And then notice, that you, as a note, have an exact counterpart on the adjacent scale up the keyboard, and another one adjacent to that, and so, on it goes.

Now, realize that you as a Spirit, have a specific note, on the scale of your 3rd dimensional reality, and that other notes that are you, intrinsically you, reside in higher realms of existence than this one.

So, essentially, your ascension is your movement to a different scale, while still staying the note that you have always been. And as this same note within the new scale of the 4th and 5th dimensional reality, you will find an awareness that shares with you vistas of the wide range of the scales you partake in as a note, all the way up to the Source of all there is: **the Great Central Sun**.

And so, you will embrace the multidimensional being that you are, and you will resonate with joy across all aspects of your being, across all the scales there are and ever have been in the infinite reality of all there is.

The Energy Body

We will now provide a brief introduction to your energy body, your aura and your chakras. This will give you the information you need to choose a particular section of the book to open up a particular area of your body, or to heal a particular issue. For each section and each written piece of the book heals a different part of your energy body.

And so, now, we ask you take a look at your body. Do you like it? Do you think it could be better shaped, better formed or more in tune with your inner vision of yourself? Well, we ask you to consider the fact that just as you would like to improve your physical body, get it more in shape, get it more in tune with where you would wish to be, so it is that your physical body is only a small component of your overall body, a large part of which is invisible to the physical eye. And these invisible parts of the body must also be tuned, attuning them to the possibilities of the ascension, and of going home to the heart of **God/Goddess**, the Creator, the Source of all there is.

In this book, in certain pieces, we refer to the **PEMS body**. This is an acronym for Physical, Emotional, Mental and Spiritual Body. For you exist in a continuum, and the part of the continuum that is manifested as you in this 3rd dimensional reality, or holograph that we call planet Earth, or Gaia, is comprised of your physical body which you can see, an invisible body surrounding that that contains many emotions, fears and joys, that we call the emotional body, another invisible body surrounding the emotional body, which is the source of many of the ideas and thoughts that pop into your head, and then there is the spiritual body, that connects you, provides the bridge, so to speak, to the aspects of you with exist in the higher dimensions.

When clairvoyants talk about the colors of your aura, and, when, indeed, you take pictures of your aura, using Kirlian photographic techniques, you are, in a sense capturing only a small portion of your non-physical body, which is mostly your emotional body. There are certainly aspects of your emotional, mental and spiritual bodies that exist outside of your perceivable aura.

Can this be possible you ask? Well, we ask you to consider the notion that everything about you, as a consciousness, is energy. You are Spirit, you are energy. And you materialized as a body into this 3rd dimensional earth as energy. The physicality of your body is an illusion. The cells and atoms of your body are mostly space. There is a central nucleus core within each atom, but then the surrounding electrons seem to be diffuse, almost dancing here and there, depending on how you look at them. You almost can't pin them down, in a sense. That is because at the subatomic level, all is dancing energy, and the atoms that are created are, in a sense, standing waves. If you move the electrons fast enough, they will appear to be particles, especially when you as humans try to observe them. We draw the analogy, as other channels have done, to the blades of a rotating fan.[2] If it moves fast enough, it will appear to be fixed, static, solid.

And so it is that you manifested your body as a spirit, as a holographic standing wave, with electrons and atoms moving fast enough to provide the illusion of being static. And so it is also with every other body you meet, with every other animal you meet, with every inanimate object you meet, with every aspect of nature you interact with, with every aspect of your reality. It is all a holograph of energy, fully conscious, maintained by you and many other humans, in their higher aspects to create this game of duality, so that you could all experience yourself as separate from your God-selves, so that you could experience emotions that are distinct from universal love and unity, such as fear, aloneness, greed, dissolution.

Well, you have done such a great job at this that you truly feel completely alone in the Universe; at times as agnostics, as atheists. Or, you have sometimes gone in the opposite direction, creating projected Gods in monotheistic and polytheistic traditions, creating external monoliths of power, and giving up your rights, your desires and wants to external rules that no longer make sense to you, as religious ritual has often been used to constrain humanity and perpetuate the illusion that they are alone, separate, sinful, needing redemption.

As everything about you is energy, you have stored in your **PEMS body**, many energy patterns over time, across many of your incarnations, of debilitation, of fear, of the belief that you will never have a good life, that you are alone, that you are a victim of fate, of circumstances, that somehow you deserve the miserable life you are leading, the family that does not understand you, the spouse who has grown distant from you, the children that were never grateful for the parenting you offered them.

Well, at this time of ascension, of the raising of the frequency of the energy of this planet, Gaia, to a fourth and fifth dimensional consciousness, it is time now to release any and all fears and thoughts of debilitation which are of a lower vibration, a denser vibration.

This will happen automatically, my dear ones, with the light waves that are rapidly spilling into your holographic reality. But this book provides you with another tool to raise your vibration, to heal yourself into the light of higher vibrations of energy.

Every piece written in this book, through its words and vibrations, connects with parts of your energy bodies that hold a certain belief system and pattern. And in touching this piece of yourself, with the vibration of Spirit, with the truth of how things really are, we remind the inner consciousness within you of the truth, we give you the permission to start waking up, to release the pieces, the particle of energy that have constrained you, that have held you down, that have stopped you from seeing the Creator-God that you really are, across all time and space.

And so your body will change over time, your emotions will become sunnier over time, your thoughts will becomes more positive over time, as the connection, the bridge to your Spiritual body and to higher, multidimensional aspects of yourself grows through the healing that is coming through at this time of the Shift of consciousness, and that is facilitated by the divine words of wisdom, truth, love and light contained in this book.

And we, the Spirit beings that have worked together, with our channel, Shariq, in this book, are excited at this unique collaboration that we have put together. When we have worked together to write certain pieces, we have melded our energies to provide insights that work at many frequencies of vibration, allowing us to touch different patterns of debilitation within each one of you, for in combining our energies, we expand the range of humanity that we can talk to, that we can address.

The range of Spirits working on this book is vast, and a table of Spirit authors for each piece has been provided, in Appendix 2, that will allow you to understand the range of Spirit vibrations working.

And you might find that certain pieces of this book call to you again and again. And that is a clue, my dearest one, that you have a relationship already, in the higher planes, with the Spirits that call to you with their words. So notice which pieces you like, and use this as a clue for which guides you will call to, as your PEMS body starts to open up, and as you start connecting with your multidimensional self, becoming clairvoyant, becoming yourself a channel for Spirit, and for your higher aspects of self.

The Journey of This Spiritual Path

At this time of the Shift in Consciousness to the Golden Age of being, one where you, as a Spirit in a human body, will finally begin to recognize that you are grand, glorious and that what had seemed a reality was actually an illusion of playing small, we provide this book to you as a tool, a roadmap so to speak for your own ascension.

For ascension, at this time, is about bringing your Spirit, your higher dimensional aspects of self into your body, and allowing your body, your physical being to recognize that it is indeed part of the unified Spirit that animates all, that is Source.

To facilitate this, you must use the winds of change, and the lightwaves of change to first cleanse your PEMS body of all cultural and ancestral and past life programming that tells you that life is brutish, short, meaningless and that you are a victim to fate and circumstances. As you do this, you will start creating space for higher dimensional aspects of you, that can start filling in the vacuums that have been left behind.

And, so, piece by piece, you begin weaving a new you across your multiple bodies, finding that golden bridge through your Spiritual body to you spiritual self, one that is infinite, ever-present, ever-loving, all-knowing, and compassionate in its union and communion with all there is.

This book provides you with a journey of cleansing your PEMS body of pictures and programming of debilitation by escorting you, chakra by chakra to a process of self-recognition and self-alignment with your divine nature.

For your divine nature is one that is aligned with truth, beauty, colors, sounds, smells and flight, all the weavings of that which is ethereal, of that which is Source.

And so, we use the chakras of your body to align you one by one with the Nature that is around you, with the colors of life, with the patterns of sounds, of smells, of beauty, of taste all around you, leading you to your own flight into your divine destiny of reclaiming the Master that you already are, as this game of duality is now rapidly ending.

What are the chakras, you might ask. Your body, at the time of this experiment in 3rd dimensional dualistic consciousness, was designed with seven major vortexes, or spinning spirals of energy across your bodies. They correspond to certain physical locations in your body, but extend also as multidimensional cones across your PEMS body, and beyond, connecting you to multidimensional aspects of yourself as well, if you will choose to allow it.

This book is structured as an awakening and cleansing process for each of your chakras, starting at the root chakra and moving to the crown chakra and the geometries of creation that unfold from there. As we work on each of your chakras, through the pieces and words of truth and wisdom in this book, we unwind patterns of lower vibrations, belief systems that you have held onto for a very long time.

Root Chakra

And it is important to start off with the root chakra, for this is where you have stored your deepest fears, of being killed, of being hurt, of not surviving life, of being victimized by others. This is the foundation for future growth, and it must be addressed, it must be cleansed, in order to open up your third eye, your crown chakra, your connection to Spirit. Remember, that this ascension is about bringing Spirit into your body, not about leaving your body.

The root chakra is located physically at the base of your spine, and spins out as vortexes of energy in two directions from the front and back of your spine. Physically it ties into the nerve ganglia through your spine that affect your legs, genitalia and urinary and rectal problems.

For, every time we lower the frequency of our chakras, by putting another picture of fear into our space, we find ourselves reducing the light coming into our bodies, allowing disease and dis-ease to plague us. For those of you with knee, leg and other lower body problems, this is a good sign that your root chakra has some cleansing work to be done.

So we start off this book, in **Chapter 1, Colors for Awakening**, with a series of color meditations and visualizations meant to allow your bodies to vibrate at higher resonances of alignment with your spirit selves. For as you start focusing on the fact that you are indeed grander and larger than you have ever allowed yourself to believe that you are, you find that some of the pictures of fear, anger and depression start leaving your space very easily.

As you awaken to who it is you really are, you will automatically start moving from your space, those pictures of debilitation and fear stored through your root chakra all across your bodies.

So, if you have a fear that you might die in a plane crash, you might keep manifesting situations whereby you choose flights in thunderstorms, and you find yourself sitting next to passengers who are themselves jittery, amplifying the emotional pictures of fear in your emotional body via resonance.

And, then, you think that something really bad is going to happen, in your Mental body, and your Emotional body grows another picture of fear, all coordinated by the frequency of survival fear, tuned into by your root chakra, and so the plane suddenly takes another lurch towards unpredictability.

Well, dear ones, **Chapter 2, Flying to Your Destiny,** is meant to start showing you, through the truth of the words that are written, that you are like a bird in your flight, you are completely in control of every journey you take, and you can have calm weather, wonderful company and a first class seat if you want, on every step of your journey, on every flight that you choose to embark on, in your life. So breathe deep, and exhale dear ones, for this chapter will teach your root chakra, will let your root chakra remember that you are a Master, that you are not only the pilot, but that you are also a designer for the spacecraft. And so you can change your reality at any time by changing the pictures of fear stored within your root chakra, and so create a new glorious life.

And, as in any pattern of debilitation, although themes, like fear of survival for the root chakra, are centered in certain locations in the body, the pattern is often complex, and extends to many other parts of the PEMS body, including other chakras. This is why you will find that in Chapters 1 and 2 we work on multiple chakras, but the function overall is to start the process of helping you release fear, by focusing on the truth of that you already are, as you take flight once again.

Sacral Chakra & Solar Plexus Chakras
And as you start releasing the fear paradigm that has gripped humanity for centuries, you start giving yourself permission to explore your own tastes for creativity, fun, sensuality and joy. For, you, as a divine being, have an infinite desire and taste for creation. You have the ability to create fantastic new adventures for yourself, to manifest wonderful works of art and science, and to express your joy and fun-loving nature with others.

Here again, though, you will find that you often stop yourself from trying to learn or remember a certain skill, from dating a certain person, from taking time out to have fun because of certain beliefs that you have about responsibility, about what is right or wrong, what you ought to do, how you should taste life, how you should restrain yourself, how you should be a good person by conforming to the rules of society, often taught to you by your parents.

Your sacral chakra, located physically in the lower abdomen is the center of your creative self as you express your wonderful ideas and thoughts to the world with joy, and it is also the center of your sexuality, the permissions and inhibitions that surround your choices to taste the fruits of inhibition or of letting go, to nurture yourself with something that is tangy and interesting, or something that is boring and bland.

And so, in **Chapter 3, The Fruits of Transformation**, we begin the process of opening your sacral chakra up to the notion that permission to be yourself is quite all right. We use the fruits available in nature to share with you the knowledge that all the abundance already exists, all the different tastes in this wonderful world already exist. You just have to give yourself permission to taste them, to have fun, to overcome programming that never exposed you to certain fruits.

And as you do this, you will tread along a path of your life with ease and joy and a sensuality that will make others turn and look at you, for you are proud of yourself and your body. For the joy in life that you exhibit and radiate will draw others to you, allowing you to find opportunities to express yourself with joy and abandon.

And so it is that in **Chapter 4, Colors for Growth**, we provide you with additional colors to continue to cleanse your sacral and solar plexus chakras of limitations, giving yourself permission to release programming about how you should spend your life, who you should marry, who you should associate with. And, as you release these patterns of miscomprehension, more light continues to flood your lower body, giving you the strength and solidity to grow the base for the spiritual growth that is rapidly approaching you.

The solar plexus chakra is located physically in the solar plexus region of your body and is an expression of your will as spirit, how you choose to walk down your adventurous path in life: choosing jobs and professions that constrain you and make you miserable or those that bring you joy and allow you to be your creative self as a Spirit in a body.

Do you let your fear of lack of money hold you back in a perpetual state of poverty consciousness, or do you let yourself believe that abundance and prosperity is your divine right, whatever choice you make, as long as it brings you joy?

And so, as you claim the mastery within, as you claim your divine right to creatively express your life with joy, you will also find that any physical ailments related to stomach problems, lower back pains, womb issues for women, will start receding. For your physical symptoms are but the physical manifestations of lower vibrating, fear-based thought forms that start in your emotional and mental bodies, dropping down to your physical, as the patterns become all-encompassing.

And we pass no judgment on what you created before, both in this lifetime and in other prior lifetimes, pictures of which are also stored within your PEMS body. For, you were playing a game of duality, one where the karmic wheel often brought you the same patterns and experiences of limitation again and again, until you learned the lesson.

What a wonderful game you set up for youselves, dear ones, to believe that it had to be so. Well the time now affords you the opportunity to change all that, to break the karmic wheel as you begin to spriral up instead, to your own rapidly approaching ascension to higher vibrations of being.

Heart Chakra

As we have worked on opening up and healing the root, sacral and solar plexus chakras, so it is that you are now prepared in **Chapter 5, Flowering into the Perfumes of Self-Awareness**, to breath in the sacred beauty and light that informs and conforms to your true, divine god-self that is perfectly attuned to the vibrations of compassion, union and communion with your fellow brethren, with humanity as a whole.

And so it is that in this chapter, we use the beauty of the vibrations of flowers and the smells of splendor that they share in their blooming to alight within you the knowledge of the flowering of your own connection to your Higher Self, to your god-self.

And, as you read through the poetry of love and compassion that we weave in this section, you will continue to open your heart to infinite and compassionate love: love for yourself, for your community and for humanity as a whole.

And, as this occurs, you will empower yourself to release the wounding, the alignment to vibrations of fear, worry and debilitation that kept you mired in isolation and rejection, allowing you to falsely believe that you were not worth much, that you did not deserve love, in relationship, in community, with humanity.

And with the tears of sorrow for the illusion that has been you awaken to your own spring and blooming and you flower into your new self-awareness of your God-Self. And from the sacred heart chamber, with it infinite dimensions, that you uncover, you will find many pathways of connections, in new ways with those you have known before and those who you will draw to you now with your higher vibrations of love. You will find the right ones for you to commune with, as you choose with discernment what makes your garden bloom.

And within the core of your being, you will flower into a wonderful emblem of compassion that is Christ consciousness, the source of strength and community, the source of unity, the Source of all.

Throat Chakra & Third Eye Chakra
Most of the time, we feel like there is no end to the miseries of life. Most of the time, we feel like there is no end to the deprivation, of the lack of understanding of our overall path and mission.

Well, dearest ones, we move now, with the clearing of your root, sacral and solar plexus chakras, and the re-firing of the sacred love for self and for community within your heart chakra, we move to the three chakras that help attune you to higher frequencies of yourself, the three chakras that find you the pathway home, that lead you to your ascension: the throat chakra, the third eye chakra and the crown chakra.

Within **Chapter 6, Growing Out of the Nest**, we start training you, with the vibration of the words we have written, to understand that since all of your atoms and cells are dancing to a particular vibration, it is in your interest to move that vibration to one that represents you in your entirety, one that is your divine vibration.

And the way you do this is to release past programming and vibrations in your cells of being a victim to circumstances. You give up the waiting for someone to save you. And, instead, you find your own songs, your songs of that information that is divine, provided through the clairaudience of your guides and your Higher Self.

You create a new antenna so to speak, and indeed, you do speak in a new way, for as you trust your inner guidance more and more, your throat chakra opens more, the sound of your voice becomes firmer, more certain, and the timbre of that sounds you emit retrain your cells to claim the hero within, and in sharing your wisdom, your thoughts and your insights with others, you will entrain them as well to grow, to fly out of their nests and make their own chirpings, if they are ready, and if they so choose.

As your throat chakra expands, it might encounter turbulence in the flight we have been advocating. For, there is much deep programming within your cells about the dances and vibrations that are allowed; programming that comes from your cultural milieu, from your religious upbringing, or lack of it, and from your genetic ancestry. It is this turbulence that we address head on, in **Chapter 7, The Fruits of Amelioration**, where we encourage you to bite into the tastes of manna, of that which is medicinal, of that which will cure you of past inhibitions and limitations, allowing you to find the Milky Way, the galaxy of knowledge within, as you connect with your source of all divine knowledge and information.

And as you claim this mantle, as you express your truth with the specific vibrations that you embody in your body, you will find your physical voice getting stronger, you will find less propensity for sore throats, and you will breathe deeper into your sacred heart.

For, as you taste yourself more and more, you will banish, with the unconditional love that you feel for all, any physical ailments surrounding separation from Source or community such as asthma and heart disease.

And so you will build a new community, one that hears your true divine voice and resonates with it. And those who do not want to listen to you might fall away from your life, and that is ok. They might reconnect with you later, as they themselves grow. Hold your light, and spread your truth, and others might taste the fruits of amelioration that have helped you grow and overcome doubts.

And you will find in this book now that the pieces become more intricate, the metaphors more extended, as we extend the weavings and patterns of the new you that we are spinning with the words, the expressions of divine truth and the Word, the logos of all there is, in this book.

And just like this world of yours was manifested into form through the vibration, the logos, the breath and sounding of Source, so it is that with the soundings of the healings contained within these chapters, you will continue to recreate yourself, allowing for a golden rebirthing into the colors of a divinity within.

For, all light, that proceeds from the love of creation, is a frequency. And every frequency has a color. So, now, as you move to higher frequencies of understanding and vibration, so it is that in **Chapter 8, Colors for Divining**, we provide colors and frequencies to awaken your third eye chakra, located in the center of your forehead, and fired by the pineal gland inside your head. We lead you step by step to your higher alignments of the patternings of the self.

And, as each color washes over you, you begin to understand the alchemical potentials of the inner magician and wizard within. For you, as the expression of God on Earth, already know how to create, for you created this reality. And, in the colors for divining, we give you the tools, the mantras, to color your clairvoyance, your ability to co-create your future, the ability to completely change your reality, into manifested form.

And so, you find the eye of Horus growing within the center of your forehead, you find yourself flowering into higher and higher vibrations in the garden that you have created within your body, as a new red rose of the understanding of the high frequencies of unconditional love for all of humanity, takes hold.

Along the way, though, there will be times when you feel constrained, when you feel like the growth is taking you backwards, regressing you to experience once again all those fears you thought you had left behind. Do not be worried, dear ones. This sense of confinement is part of the process of growth, of accepting, of claiming your experiences of duality, and as you accept your life's experiences with gratitude, you break through a new vista of understanding, a new vista of consciousness.

Crown Chakra
As you now center yourself in the love that you are, as you find and uncover the truth that you are infinite, you will indeed find that unconditional love fires the light that burnishes a golden crown across your head, a golden crown that reflects a new crown chakra that is opening at the top of your head, like a 1,001 petalled lotus, connecting to aspects of yourself that are infinite, and always have been, and always will be.

In **Chapter 9, Geometric Flowerings of Consciousness**, we align you to the truth of your love for yourself and for all of creation. We align you to the truth that as you are rebirthed into golden consciousness, you will begin to access aspects of understanding that share with you the truth that all of Nature, including your nature, unfolds from the grand divine design that is simple in its growth patterns, according to the number and geometry of that which is harmonious, that which is aligned with higher divine truth, love and knowledge.

And so it is, that we explain and introduce the concepts of the spiracular growth of plants and flowers, the golden ratios contained within the Fibonnaci sequence that drives growth in this Universe that you inhabit, and, in so doing, we remind you not only of the knowledge of creation that you already find contained within the very core of your being as a Creator-God, but we also align you with your own sense of communion with community and all of Nature, for your nature is indeed part of all of Nature, is indeed part of unity, from whence you came.

And, as you understand the context of this game you have played, within the many lifetimes you have experienced on this Earth plane, you will rediscover the tri-fold flame within your sacred heart, that connects you to the source of all that you are.

And what you are is an expression of infinite creative consciousness, that in awakening now, and refiring your crown of higher geometric understandings of unity consciousness, are being called to service, to align your bodies to the heavenly changes of the Shift, to the geometric grids of change surrounding your planet, so that you can radiate out your truth, your infinity, your geometry, aligning others and allowing others to flower into their own awakenings of higher consciousness.

In **Chapter 10, The Fruits of Ascension**, we begin sharing with you the higher divine wisdom that is the Universal Mind. We share with you the concepts of simultaneous time, the possibilities for connecting to Higher aspects of your self via the axiotonal lines of connection that are growing through the 144-faceted crystalline grid surrounding your planet that is geometrically shining the light of love through a crystalline formation, allowing your planet to ascend to higher realms of understanding and the New Age of enlightenment.

And we share with you the knowledge of the simplicity of all of creation, for indeed you already know this deep down inside your sacred heart. We share with you the importance of the patterning within the geometry of all there is, as the infinity of self-replication of creation results in the fractal nature of Nature, leading to geometric alignments and concatenations where resonance allows for infinity to connect with infinity across all space and time.

And so, you are prepared for your divine destiny, anchoring in the seeds of understanding that will take you on the next legs of your infinite journey within simultaneous time, back to the heart of God/Goddess, back to the heart of yourself.

And, as you do, you will find not only your head becoming lighter, not only your eyesight increasing in its ability to perceive all that is solid, and also all that is ethereal and infinite, but you will also find that you are developing a new body, one that is lighter, one that conducts the love and light of the geometries of color, sound, taste and smell, allowing you to fly to higher dimensional realities while still in a body that is reconstituted, reconfigured with more of your DNA and RNA strands activated than ever before, as you vibrate at higher frequencies of light and love.

The Stained Glass Merkaba

And so it is that we share the divine truth with you, that the process of unfolding your consciousness, by partaking of the journey of the words and sounds and patterns of this book, will unveil for you what has always existed around you: a **merkaba** of crystalline glass, that you are re-activating through the colors, sounds, tastes and smells that this book provides. It is a merkaba that allows you traverse the history of yourself and of the cosmos.

And it is your unique geometrically patterned merkaba, arranged geometrically around you in a particular 3-D configuration that reflects your particular infinite soul signature and taste and smell and mix of colors.

See yourself now emanating light from the center of your sacred heart, through the love that you are, and this light illuminates this geometrically complex crystalline merkaba situated and aligned in your particular vibration all around your body. And then celebrate the beautiful, multi-colored, geometrically unique stained glass shell of connection to all there is that you have uncovered around yourself.

This book has not constructed it for you, for it was always there. We have merely helped to shine the light on all the illusions that kept you form seeing the infinity and expression of the Creator that you have always been. We trust you will enjoy the journey back to the heart of your inner God/Goddess.

We are, Ra, Kuthumi, Mother Mary, Hathors & Archangel Gabriel on behalf of all the Spirit Collaborators for this book.

Root Chakra
Maple Tree—Rooting Yourself to Your Inner Joy

Someone once said: "You have to sit under a tree, like a Buddha, to gain insightful knowledge, to understand the true meaning of it all." Well, perhaps, not those exact words, but you get the gist. Many people are told that they must study hard, and spend months, if not years, in meditation, seeking to attain divine knowledge, to gain wisdom, to learn the way of the Buddha, out of **Samsara**.

But the irony is that each one of you is already a Buddha, and that the simplest way of achieving your mastery and accessing your divine self is to breathe and believe in yourself. It lies not in sitting endlessly under a tree meditating. It lies in recognizing that the tree of life, the tree of divine revelation and connection lies within your very human frame. And it takes the form of chakras within your body that connect with the larger parts of you, filtering energy to you at an etheric level.

And so we begin this book with a series of metaphors about the chakras in your body, with each chakra represented by a tree. And this is significant because as you come to a recognition of the larger tree that your body is, connecting your human frame like an antenna to the Universal cosmos of all there is, you also begin to understand that each cell within your body, and, indeed, each chakra is itself a macrocosm of beauty, is itself a mini-tree of infinite understanding and knowledge.

And hence we look at the maple tree as a metaphor for the Root chakra.

Picture yourself as a child of five years old, unharried by life, living in the moment, full of joy and excitement about your day. You planned to spend time doing the things you loved. Perhaps it was dancing, perhaps it was singing, perhaps it was simply running around, being silly. And as you attempted to simply be playful and enjoy your human moment, you fulfilled a part of you that wanted to be joyful and was unrestrained.

And so you bloomed inside like a flower, the red rustic sheen of health spreading across your cheeks with a flush of excitement as you realized that nothing could be more fun than being free, enjoying the moment.

And so we would like to compare this freedom that you experienced once, and might have given up a bit as an adult, to the beautiful colors, in the fall, of the maple tree. Its bright oranges and reds and yellow express the beauty, the magnificence of Nature. There is a growing sense of awe when one sees the spreading colors of the maple tree as it celebrates its season "of mellow fruitfulness"[3].

And, as your cheeks get flushed with excitement, you, too, are expressing the inner divine joy of simply recognizing the magnificence of who you are in your physical body. This is a body you chose, that you never could have experienced as a timeless, infinite spirit, and so you celebrate its movement, its voice, its athleticism.

And it is within the root chakra, located at the base of your spine, and pulsating and spinning in a red *joie de vivre* of color, that you find the closest association between the divine and the human skeleton, flesh and cells that ever has existed. This is the point, the nexus of the complete immersion of your divine soul into the solid matter of flesh.

So, as you contemplate your root chakra now, in its red, divine glory, we ask you to set an intention, a prayer if you wish, as you go forward to read this book. Ask that any fears stored in your body, in your root chakra, about limitation, fear, survival, hunger, bodily injury all be released by the words and energy that comes forth. Ask to focus you attention instead on the beautiful, limitless joy of enjoying the body that you inhabit.

Take a moment now to thank yourself for having chosen your specific body. For having chosen your specific face, your specific hair, your specific hands and feet, your specific body shape and height, your specific sexual organs. For each part of you is perfect. It is for the experience of this specific body that you have come to Earth. And this moment, this creation of this body, with its ancestral and DNA lineage will never be repeated in time.

So enjoy this lifetime, celebrate this lifetime. Celebrate your body. And let the sweetness of maple syrup spread all through your body, seeping out from the maple tree of your root chakra, converting every single cell from a vibration of fear and limitation to a vibration of love and infinite joy at the experiences that you are creating by being alive.

And let the red love of the red rose, of the pure divine fire that burns within all, rise through your body like a fire of **kundalini**, bringing, to your face, the red flush of joy and a purposeful life, where your dreams come true.

And with this vibration, now turn the page and start the journey toward a fuller recognition of who you really are.

Chapter 1
Colors for Awakening

Gold—*Know Your Intrinsic Value*

Gold has always been a value of last resort. Whenever things are down and the value of everything is topsy-turvy, gold has been the last denominator: that which you can always hold onto, that which will always be exchangeable for something else, that which makes you feel rich.

In ancient times, kings and governments would measure their wealth and status by the amount of bullion in their coffers. And until the end of the Depression, the Gold Standard, where gold backed the value of all major currencies in the world, was sacrosanct, unlike today where paper money is given much more value than the paper it is printed on.

Surround yourself now, dear ones, with a beautiful golden mist of your intrinsic value, of your beauty which never falters, never loses its sense of self or achievement. Visualize this golden mist swirling all around you and settling down over your face, body, arms, legs, torso. It covers you up and you, like the gilded statues of old, become the ebullient trophy of your magnificent Higher Self. You are golden in every way, and your bust, your gilded statue celebrates your unique authenticity and flavor.

You move your arms and legs, and are surprised to find that you are not constricted. For this gilding on your skin is not limiting. In fact, it empowers you into action, as you are spurred by an inner strength that you never dared believed that you truly possessed. You are golden sunshine personified into a gilded human expression.

Shine your golden glory into the world, knowing you will never lose your value, knowing that through any Depression, you will be able to weather the storm, that no matter what others think of you, as you show them your gilded self they will want more of you, for they will begin to value you. As you value yourself and gild yourself, you will grow in stature.

Green—*The Emerald Light of Unity*

Emerald green light pierces and permeates the pure of heart. The light of emerald green love emits with beauty from your heart chakra when you are aligned with the divine will of the Creator.

Imagine yourself spilling forth brilliant emerald green light from your heart chakra now out into your surroundings, out into your aura, out into the very space that defines you. Feel the green mist of love and purity cleanse your very being. Change the color to apple green and feel the juicy taste of what is recommended by doctors for you every day. Nourish yourself with this love, this purity.

And others will know that you are a being of integrity, a being of compassion, one who understands that all the others are not separate, are not just someone else, but part of that very whole that you come from. You shine your brilliant emerald green light and bite into the luscious green apple of Source that sustains and is everything.

Feel yourself now connected to your loved ones, your family, your neighbors, your city dwellers, to the citizens of your country, to the citizens of your world, to the citizens of your Universe and beyond.

Realize that everything you do affects someone else, and that there is nothing you can do without the support of someone else.

Others have helped make you who you are. And you help others develop and grow by shining your emerald beauty out to them.

Unity. Oneness. Source.
Om. Shanti.

Pink—*An Airy Sweetness of Awareness*

Have you ever drunk pink lemonade? It has a similar taste to regular lemonade, but the addition of the pink name and color gives it some extra pizzaz. One feels the pink liquid entering one's body and providing a soothing vibration, a relaxing of the body and of the sentiments.

So we say unto you that pink is the color of softness, of sweetness, of the very divine aspect of your Creator self that finds its expression of ethereality in the material plane. Pink ribbons, pink carnations, pink roses. They all sound so wonderful and light and airy, don't they?

Well, you are light and airy and refined deep within your spiritual core. So imagine if you will a fountain of pink energy emerging now from the top of you crown chakra, at the top of your head, spilling down in it ethereality all around your body and aura, spiraling up and around you, convincing you that you are an airy spirit, Ariel, in Shakespeare's magical play "The Tempest". You, like Ariel now, can flit and float across the trees, across the landscape, across the world, across the many different worlds and dimensions.

For with this pink light of enlightenment and discernment that now lights up your physical, emotional and mental bodies, you become a Master of piercing the veils of mystery. You become adept at that which you have always been adept at beyond time and space. You merge with the oneness of your Creator self and find yourself and your many aspects in full glorious pink regalia.

And you breathe the sweet perfume of a pink rose. Of a pink carnation. And you sip that pink lemonade knowing that you have something extra special, extra pink nourishing you. And you bloom and grow and expand in your expanded awareness.

Yellow—*The Beam Leading You To Your Destiny*

Yellow is the color of happiness, of natural daffodils, of sunny temperaments and a lightness of being.

Yellow is the attention that one pays to one's path, just as Dorothy did down the yellow brick road[4].

Yellow is also a symbol of hope, leading us to our destiny, to our potential, allowing us to live a life of joyous passion, as we learn to truly experience the magnificent beings that we are.

And so, if you are feeling down, if you want to break through the brick walls around you and transform them into a yellow brick path that leads you to your destiny, imagine a beautiful yellow light coming down to you from the sunny sky, full of the fresh smells of budding daffodils.

Imagine this light as a cone enveloping your entire body in a snug cocoon of comfort and bliss. And breathe deeply. Inhale the divine, powerful self that you are, and resolve to take the next step on your path, in line with your intuition, in line with the passion that you feel for life and your journey.

Take the next step knowing that you will be divinely guided and protected by this shining beam showing you your path.

Caramel—*Bringing out the Sweetness in Yourself*

When I think of caramel, I think of food deliciously sweet, sugary, melting and full of delight. The suffix 'mel' has a latin root, as in molasses, of sweetness, of light[5]. Molasses have been a symbol of heavenly manna in many traditions. So think, as you eat your caramel pudding, or you caramelize some sugar for a recipe, that you are creating a part of God's incredible sweetness. You are bringing out the sweetness in yourself and tasting it.

And just like caramel can take on many consistencies: a little airy in a pudding, crunchy in a toffee, or just a flavor in an ice cream, you too can express your caramel sweetness in many ways. You can offer yourself as a loving consciousness to others, willing to support and affirm the other in your own special, unique way, flowing in a way to accommodate others. You can be the solid, tasty, crunchy caramel providing the foundation for a dish, allowing others to build on your base, creating a whole of exquisite taste. And you can be your own special flavor, full of unknown whiffs and caramel scents.

Use the caramel light, the caramel color, the caramel taste as an expression of your own inner divinity. Feel yourself surrounded in a sticky, sweet, caramel halo to attach yourself to the sweetness of the Creator; the sweetness of yourself.

And burn up in this divine recognition creating the sweet topping for the delicious cream underneath. For what would a crème brulee be without the caramelized sugar topping?

Orange—*The Glowing Igniter of Your Divine Self*

Orange can be tangy. Orange can be warm. Orange can be nourishing, like a shot of vitamin C from the juice that graces your morning. But let's not make orange more complicated than it needs to be. Orange is the light of a beautiful sunrise or a beautiful sunset. It is a reflection of the magnificence and beauty of the Creator. Let its light bathe you and ignite the fires within. Let the embers glow with the orange desire to combine, to become one with Source.

Take a bite from the etheric orange before you. Feel the taste of that vitamin C boost nourishing your system. Let it pervade all of your being, nourishing each and every cell. Let this orange miasma ignite the embers of remembrance in every cell of your body, reawakening that part of your DNA that is divine, that part of your DNA that is eternal, that part of your DNA that is all-knowing.

As you glow now in your divine self-knowledge, you are complete, and your embers reflect their rays of happiness and abundance to others, creating the fire in the grate of their homes that warms them as you glow in your own glory.

Repeat this mantra aloud to yourself as you visualize being of service to others:

I send my glowing love to you with an open heart.
May my embers and heat ignite your very core,
Igniting in you your very own sunrise.
And if ever there is a beautiful sunset,
Know that another glowing sunrise is but a few hours away.

Blue—*A Regal Expression of the Authentic Self*

There is a saying that "I'm feeling blue", as if to say that blue means sad, depressed, neglected. Refocus this notion. Blue is a regal color of your strength, your wisdom, your inherent creativity, your beautiful, magnificent expression of your authentic self.

Imagine as you speak out loud, the uniqueness of your voice and your vibration is expressed in that particular shade of regal blue that is only you. It is a blue cloud of your voice that envelops your throat chakra now, imbuing you with that divine sense of certainty that your expression is one of clarity, hope and a vision that is particular to your very special journey.

As this blue color spins around your throat chakra you feel an angelic sense of release, of freedom, never to be afraid again to speak your truth, to express how you feel. Never again let anyone else tell you that what you say is not valid, that you should not have said it. If you said it, then it is your expression and you should own it.

The one exception is when you feel the energies of anger, jealousy, envy, or rage. Whenever you feel such an energy taking hold of your body, choose not to react; choose not to speak out loud for 20 minutes, while those destructive energies dissipate.

And while you wait, call on Napoleon's blue color of liberation[6], feel it enveloping your entire body and clearing your throat chakra of the dross, as you drink in the nectars of the Universe.

Later, you will express your authentic sense again in all your glory. For when you speak while angry or while consumed by destructive energies, you are cut off from your authentic self, and you speak what is not your truth.

If you are "feeling blue" in the angry or depressed sense, call on your Creator to help refine this blue to your royal, regal, Napoleonic blue of victory and accomplishment. And then let the world hear your magnificence. For you are a light being of immense power, knowledge and beauty. Recognize yourself, reclaim it, and express it.

Purple—*Astounding Awareness*

Astounding, isn't it? You look at the color purple and you want to scream in abundance, in abeyance, and in royalty. The color confuses you. It is dark, yet it is rich. It is succulent, like a plum, yet it is murky, like still water. It is this complexity in reaction that creates a craving in you for more. It excites you and repels you at the same time. Astounding, isn't it?

So dear ones, when you are feeling stupefied by life, when you are feeling that things are not going your way, imagine your crown chakra spinning above your head and churning out the astounding purple color of Source, of the creator, of that which encompasses all. Let this purple rain fill all around your aura, lifting you from the frequency of being stupefied, to the frequency of being rarefied. You find yourself breathing in purple adamantine particles into your frame which alight the brightness and blight the murkiness within. For these particles of the Creator touch the part of the creator in you, instructing your cells to spin out of your space, that which is dross, that which has been static, that which is not in motion.

For you, dear one, are always in motion, for you are always growing as a soul. To be still, to be static, is anathema to the soul, as the experience of life is everything, and is what propels your growth.

Whenever you feel like you are mired down into the pale purple mists of static, spin a royal purple rain out of your crown chakra into your space, into the DNA of your cells, reminding yourself that you are so much more than you think, that you are connected to the Creator, that you are a purple minion of the larger cosmic entity that is the universal consciousness. And this self awareness is facilitated by the higher frequencies alighted by purple rain.

Endless static becomes transformed into endless growth. For infinity has no beginning and no end. And in the higher frequencies this awareness encompasses all. Let yourself grow and become aware of your role with the infinite monolith of Source.

Red—*Grounding and Expressing the Will of the Creator*

Red can be both the color of ruby grounding and the fiery will of the Universe. It is the alpha and the omega. It is the root and the sky. It encompasses all. For linearity does not exist. In our beginning is our end.

When you want to ground yourself, call on the red ray of light and visualize a brilliant, gleaming red ruby spinning and generating the divine light for you. Feel the ruby and its light anchoring into your root chakra, located at the base of your spine.

As you feel it snugly fit in, now visualize Gaia's warm, loving, energy coming up through your feet chakras. Feel the warm sensation curling up your calves, your knees, your thighs as a pulsating red energy of the Earth which makes up your physical form. As the energy reaches your root chakra, it interacts and gleams with the red ruby, forming a loop running back down your grounding cord, all the way back down to the center of the earth.

This ruby red Gaia energy now forms your solid base, your root stump, from which you can flower, reaching up to the heavens to anchor cosmic energy in your human crystal body.

Call on the divine will of the Creator, as expressed in the **First Ray of Light** and feel yourself consumed in its passion, its desire to grow, to express, to create. You might feel yourself encased in a whirlpool of swirling Creator energy charging you all around your body. And your ruby-based Gaia grounding will maintain your stability, allowing you to bring in your complete creator self, becoming a god in human form.

Turquoise—*Believe That You Are Magic*

A peacock is said to have turquoise feathers. It sounds so exotic. Turquoise. A hint of mystique, of the Orient. Turquoise has that magical, transformational quality of making something unusual appear, of bringing the extraordinary into the ordinary realm of being.

It is that admixture of blue and green, it is that indefinable sense of something grasped: that which could not have been known before, or perhaps not in the everyday world.

And so we say unto you that whenever you wish to travel to ethereal planes, to believe that there is more to your existence than simply an earthly body that must die, wrap yourself in a cloak of turquoise and let the magic do its work. Let the colors of transformations swirl around you until you find yourself transformed into that beautiful, exotic peacock that knows the way to unknown secrets through vaguely remembered pathways.

Now walk down the runway of your life, spread your turquoise-tipped feathers far and wide. For you are the alchemical portal to your own freedom from earthly incarnation. Feel your turquoise beauty attracting and manifesting a life of abundance, for you have the magical power to create your reality. From your turquoise beauty.

You have to believe you are magic. And then, indeed, nothing will stand in your way.[7]

Navy Blue—*The Ocean Warrior*

When one looks at the ocean from an ocean liner, there are waves that flow, but it is the intense blue of the ocean that attracts us and magnetizes us, in a sense, to the depth of the earth, of all there is. It gives us a sense of magnitude for this wonderful planet, and for the Universe.

The interesting thing about the oceanic blue, however, is that it can seem almost translucent during the day, when sunlight gleams through it, yet it can also seem dark, dense, a deep blue during the night, when the sun has gone away and the stars twinkle in its place.

These are the streams of life and water that are traversed by the warriors of the night, of the ocean, that look at that dark blue and find a way to keep going on their path. We are talking, of course, dear ones, of the navies of the world that float across the depths of the ocean, finding their course, finding their path through squalls, through storms, by sunlight or by the twinkling stars.

So it is appropriate that the dark navy blue color that is worn by them in their uniforms reflect that seriousness, that sense of purpose, of determination to chart the path, to traverse the oceans, to weather the storms.

And so, dear ones, whenever life seems bottomless, whenever the oceans you are being carried away on in your life, seem opaque, dense and dark, transform this density into the navy blue of the warriors of the sea. Find the strength within to not wander or meander through the ocean of life any more, but to chart the path like an arrow, in the spirit of the navy, the warriors of the sea.

For you, too, are a warrior, a warrior of the light. You have come down into this earth to spread the light of the Creator. And when you do so, you find that your starlight reflects both the dark of the oceans of life and the navy blue of your strength, your uniform, transforming what was initially dark into a celestial pattern of harmony, purpose and courage.

And you develop foresight and the ability to take charge of your life, charting your ship and your many crewmembers that represent all your different flavors and aspects, to the next sighting of land.

Mauve—*Baptize your Inner Angel*

If you were to give a drink of water to a thirsty beggar on the street, and watch the smile of satisfaction on their face, then, that sense of doing the right thing, of transcending your reality by helping another, is the vibration of mauve, a shade of transcendent purple.

In that smile, in that moment of joy and gratitude you have helped create, you change and transmute your physical nature and body into something ethereal, something light, something angelic. You find the angel within your body, and you realize that you are bigger, much bigger than you ever imagined.

So see yourself diving into a lake of mauve water, bathing in this liquid balm of angelic transcendence. Let yourself float in the water, under the open sky, nourishing your body, your soul, your angelic self.

See yourself being baptized into a loving, caring spirit living in human form. See yourself for the angel as you are, your light now shining through your body and creating ripples in the mauve lake.

For this lake is the rest of humanity. And as you float, they support you and nourish you. And as you shine your divine angelic light to them through your kindness and selflessness, you glow and develop spiritually, baptizing yourself to a higher frequency of knowledge and ascendancy.

See yourself singing a note of pure joy at this connection, at this baptism.

And now emerge, glowing like Daphne[8] from a painting, shiny new and effervescent, glowing with inner divine mauve wisdom. For you are entering a higher octave.

Chapter 2
Flying To Your Destiny

Parrot—*Messenger, Not Mimicer*

Of course, when one listens to a parrot, one thinks that any words uttered are simply mimicry; that the bird is repeating what it has heard in an unintelligent, simplistic way. The human being is too arrogant to concede that perhaps this bird is actually very intelligent, hiding its mastery behind a cloak of mimicry.

Have you not noticed how this mimicking parrot is able to string your words or phrases together in certain streams of information that convey a new meaning, a new way of looking at something to you? Sometimes, it might even come through as an insult.

For this bird is imbued with the spirit of Gaia. Gaia, our motherly planet, it's spirit essence finds expression in many creatures, and it uses the parrot in particular to convey certain messages, both personal and planetary, depending on which parrot is the instrument, and who the audience is.

So we say to you, dear ones, if you come across a parrot, pay close heed to what words it says to you. This is a message from the Earth to you. And since you are spirit in a body, a body composed of the elements of the Earth, it would behoove you to listen to this message.

In form, in body, a parrot is slim, slight. Yet it channels the greatness that is Gaia. Similarly, within your community, there might be those human beings that seem slight, slim. And, yet, unknown to others, they might channel the messages of guidance of the Universe, of the **Elohim**.

Judge not those you do not know by their physical stature. Let their true essence unfold to you through their vibration, through the tone of their voice. Then trust your inner heart as to whether the words being uttered are worth attuning to, vibrating to, unfolding yourself to.

Within our lives, at appropriate times, we will all attract a parrot to us. One that is colorful and slight, and can take many forms, the bird itself, or a being that is a friend or family member, or simply a stranger.

So look out for this parrot and pay heed to what it says—for this is a message from your guides, from your Creator, from the Universe. It is a suggestion to help you on your path. It is a way to let you know that you are never alone.

Mimicry becomes alchemy. And so it is.

Canary—*Yellow Harbinger to Your Destiny*

Know that in the instant that life takes a deadly turn, in the instant when you know that there is mortal danger ahead of you, that is when you need to find the songbird who will save you, who will sing or warble a song to alert you to the imminent dangers that you are about to be subjected to.

A yellow canary is your friend. A yellow canary is one that can pierce the air with its warbling song of mirth and of warning. It is warm, it is glowing, it is your best defence.

So how do you befriend this yellow canary? How do you find that voice of reason, that will sound the alarms when you are about the make a crucial mistake?

We say to you that let yourself be attuned to the voice of your **guides**. Let yourself be open to that inner knowledge which will always alert you when you are about to make a mis-step.

Visualize your inner sense as a yellow canary sitting on your right shoulder. It is pretty and petite and yellow and chirpy. It warbles away a beautiful song in its regular repose. But if you are about to meet a dangerous person, if you are about to enter into an alleyway that can rob you of your dignity, if you are going to treat someone in a way that you will regret later, this yellow canary, this guide, can pierce the veils of your **ego** with a whistle alarm, alerting you to take a moment to stop and think through your action again.

So program your inner yellow canary. Imagine it sitting on your right shoulder, and say out aloud: "In the name of **I AM that I AM**, I command you, my yellow canary, to find a way to alert me, to sound the alarm if I am about to mis-step from my path; if I am about to dissolve my resolve to not go down the way of disease, of that which is not in accord with my soul; if I am about to step into a path that dangerously takes me away from my destiny. Be my guardian, be the representative of Spirit to lovingly look out for me. **And so be it.**"

As you say this, the yellow canary will smile and sing a song of congratulatory embrace as it lets you know that it will always be your friend, that it will always love you, that it will always alert you and warn you of danger, either of your own making or that which is seeking you out.

For the Universe always protects and guides those who are looking for guidance, those who are looking for succor, for redress. Ask and you shall receive.

Sometimes you need to take the first step, and then leave the rest up to your yellow canary, your representative from the Universe, who will keep you on the straight and narrow. Hearken to its call, and be the representative of the Creator that you were meant to be by fulfilling your destiny.

Warble yourself into futuristic ecstasy for you, too, as you grow, turn into a yellow canary for others, alerting them to dangers as you see them take their paths. But remember, you can simply give your perspective, your truth. And then step aside and let the others make their own decisions. For this game is about making choices. That is how we learn.

Cuckoo—*A Dance to Inner Time*

Somewhere in time there exists
A plenitude, a desire to desist
The hearkenings of the daily grind;
To see through the enfolding mists.

For, you often hear the cuckoo clock
Chiming incessantly by the hour;
Reminding you of passing time,
As you pause, and try to take stock

Of where you have been and where
You are going; of how much you
Have achieved and how far there is
To go, to land, to express deeply somewhere.

And so you respond to the timely chirping
With a step of two-step, with the dance
Of movement as you move forth,
Searching for your goal, seeking, learning.

Know that your inner cuckoo
Knows more that any haste can teach.
Know that it is by listening to the chime,
By listening to its echo,

That you can discover the truth
About your journey; that you can
Let yourself be in the moment
Rather than become a sleuth,

Trying to discover the hidden
Pathways to your destiny.

So pause and reconsider and echo
The cuckoo slowly; for inspiration

Is on its way to you. It is indeed
Inside you, a part of you,
And already encoded in your being,
As you claim your certainty and take the lead.

Finch—*Into the Urban Woods We Go, Expressing Our Superlativeness*

In a sense the finch is the everyday bird on the road, on the streets of any urban landscape. A male finch's brownness, it's lack of color is, in a sense, a reflection of the spiritual unease that pervades the streets of urban clutter, where police sirens often linger oppressively in the air. Cement gardens and plastic crowns of palatial glory. Urban landscapes can wither the spirit and make us hunger for a brighter reality.

Remember dear ones, that a finch is a wonderful creation of the Creator and you should not overlook its complexity, its astounding beauty just because it is seen so commonly, just because it is a bit colorless and fits in with, shall we say, some colorless urban surroundings. For the finch is a reflection of the surroundings it is in. It wants to belong, it fits in. And yet, within the crowded urban scene, it finds time to sit on a perch, on a cornice of an office or residential building, and quietly sing a beautiful song full of wisdom, of antipathy to all that is negligent towards it, and finally, reconciliation and acceptance of a life that is wonderful in every moment, even if that very moment is fleeting and changing.

And so you too, dear one, might be the finch on an urban cornice waiting for a quiet moment to unfurl your song of joy, of trepidation, of longing for something better, of a deep understanding for your very specific situation. And instead of mulling and worrying about the future, instead of brooding about the past, use that moment to just be, and sing your song.

Sing a song of your journey, of your experience, of your creativity. Sing your special song, for even though you might feel that you are like everyone else, even though you might feel that your finch-being is just like all the other brown and colorless finch beings in a crowded, unassimilating urban landscape, you will discover in your internal journey of self-discovery how truly wonderful and unique you are.

You will discover that within that brown coating of feathers of the finch, underneath that brown or black coat you dutifully wear to keep out the cold, lies a being of light, a being of delight, a being that wants to shine a light.

So sing your song and dance your special song, dear finch-brown-urban-dweller. And take the time out to have fun within your day. Take time out to absolve yourself from the corporate misery, from the noisy sensibility that might be your everyday reality. And let yourself explore the dimensions of being that transcend the everyday, that transcend the ubiquitous and become a finch-defying superlativeness.

Ask yourself what you can be and you will know that you can be it. Ask yourself what you inner being wants to express and it will be. Let your inner self grow and sing a song within the finch armor and exterior you keep around you. And warble your inner beauty within the urban jungle you call home.

Robin—*Expressing and Experiencing Life With Abandon*

It is an ontological truth that birds must fly, that birds must be a part of the air, a part of the earth, and a part of the water. They fly through the air, they feed off the earth, and they skim over the waters of the oceans, enjoying every aspect of this beautiful Earth.

A robin is, in a sense, the quintessential expression of this avian freedom to explore and play and be happy in this vast and beautiful playground of Gaia. It is a bird that boldly goes where other birds have gone before and, sometimes, even where they might not choose to go again. For, like a wandering minstrel, the bird wishes to see what is on the other side, to explore the different aspects of creation on this planet. And, so, the robin explores the scrapings on the ground in urban areas, it pecks at pieces of flesh undulating on the water, and it flies high in the sky and chirps its song of happiness. No aspect of its experience does it shun.

We would like you, dear one, to become the robin of playfulness and happiness within your life, leaving no stone unturned in exploring the many opportunities that life sends your way. Let yourself not pre-judge any experience.

Explore the richness of the ground, the lawns, the parks, the forests, the mountains. Pick or buy the bounty that mother Nature provides you in terms of fruit and vegetables, and the occasional piece of meat from an animal that has chosen to be of service to humanity. Enjoy the taste, the sensation. Go by the water's edge and dip your feet in, like a robin might, or plunge right in and swim with the ebb and flow of the masses of water that circulate this vast Earth. And if you really want to fly, go hanggliding or jump out of an airplane. You can do it! And you will have fun.

The point is that even a small, ubiquitous robin knows how to aggressively enjoy life, to take every moment to its fullest, to expand an opportunity into a momentous experience, and this is a way of life that we would like all of humanity to embrace.

You might ask, "Well, what about all the problems in my life: the money, the shelter, the health issues, the worry about the future."

And we would say to you that go back to that robin inside you. Take a walk, meander through a park, eat a delicious fruit, smell a flower. And then go back to your daily activities refreshed. And you will find as you resume your daily routine, that a spark of inspiration will occur to you as to what the next step will be. Serendipitiously, a friend or a stranger will contact you with a suggestion or an unexpected opportunity.

Grasp these hints and guideposts that Spirit sends you with tenacity, dear one; the same tenacity that the small, red-breasted robin demonstrates in seeking out a fully lived live. And, like the robin, spread your wings and fly into your next moment. Your red feathered plumage will swell with pride and a glowing satisfaction, exhibiting that burning joy of existence in a fiery expression of the Creator in you.

Bluebird—*Noting the Blue Certainty and Taking Flight Today*

In a sense there is no time like the present to explore the opportunities for the future. What we mean by this is that you might be daydreaming often that tomorrow I will start doing this one thing that will help me become a success. The next week I will finally start taking that dance class or those yoga lessons, begin taking time out for myself. Yes, definitely, next month I will take time out for a breather, for a walk in the park.

But we say to you, dear one, happiness is not around the corner. Happiness lies in your present moment, in your today. Try to take that first step, that dance class, that yoga lesson today. And you will find that simply taking that first step towards a goal, towards your destiny, towards understanding yourself will render you happy instantaneously. For you would have started down a path towards fulfillment.

And so you start the process of transforming yourself from a human being to a multi-organic being, for as you start taking flight, you start becoming a bluebird of happiness, a bluebird of courage, a bluebird of certainty.

In the very process of taking a movement towards a destiny, a recognized path of growth, you, in a sense, start sprouting feathers and wings. And the blue color represents your royalty, your sense of ease of growth, and your certainty that all you need is to take the next step, and the rest will take care of itself.

For the bluebird, dear one, is a happy bird of courage, of multifarious abilities, and with a clear sense of direction. It knows its destiny and it knows that it will get there one step at a time, one day at a time. And it does not worry or plan for tomorrow, or the next week, or the next month.

It simply warbles its beautiful song of happiness, its notes rippling the water in the stagnant pools of desire and hope nearby, releasing the static the sense of being frozen from movement, so that the ripples create undulating blue energy circles of certainty, of royalty and of flight.

Fly on, dear ones, and transform yourself into the multi-organic, multi-faceted beings of happiness that you are all becoming as the Shift proceeds. Do not fear that you do not understand all of your destiny, or how exactly it is that you will get there. Simply tune into your intuition and take a step today that will further your growth. And the Universe will take care of the rest. Breathe and let the ease of happiness, of being in the moment totally absorb you as you warble your song outwards and send ripples of blue hope and courage and fortitude to others.

Interregnum. Encalado[9]. Freedom.

Sacral Chakra

Cherry Tree—Red Fruit and Blossoming Flowers on Display in your 2nd Chakra

Undecided you often feel, undecided about if this one is the right one for you, undecided if you should deepen a relationship, cut it off, or let it linger. And the emotions that you feel well up inside of you, burning deep, almost letting those aspects of your inner emotional core be uncovered to their red desires of lust and fulfillment.

For we all want to find the perfect lover, one who is passionate, one who is caring and tender, one who lets us express ourselves and loves us just the way we are. This is the one to whom we wish to give up our deepest hidden desires. This is the one to whom we wish to offer our inner cherry to be savored. And we search for this one again and again. We try and find this perfect match. And then we never seem to find one to live up to our standards. And so we never really offer up our inner cherry. We never really let our deepest desires be exposed. For we are afraid that we will be mocked. We are afraid of the unveiling.

And so we let the cherries inside us wither away. We never show others the beautiful flowers that can bloom in the 2nd chakra of our inner cherry tree. We hide away the beauty of our sexuality, of our sensuality. And what a waste this is!

For have you never seen the beauty of the flowering cherry tree? There is a reason the Sakura[10] is so favored in Japan. Its beauty enchants and enlivens even the most jaded person in the park. There is something so beautiful about a flowering cherry tree, in its expression of simple, joyous existence, that one cannot but smile, one cannot but be touched deep inside our core.

And so, we say to you, that in the new energies of the New Earth that are emerging, your 2nd chakra will open up more and you will let more see the true, creative, sexual you, and you will unveil the throbbing red cherries inside to those who are attracted to you. You will not wait to find an imaginary perfect partner. But you will accept that others have flaws, just like you do, and in so doing, you will uncover their particular brand of cherry tree as well, as you connect, second chakra to second chakra, creating a new union, a new cutting, a new breed.

And for those relatives and friends who, unbeknownst to you, have already tapped into the deep recesses of your 2nd chakra, and have been enjoying these hidden fruits without you knowing, sucking dry the juice inside and keeping you in the dark, so that you could not even notice that your fruit was being siphoned off, feeding others, while your own self-confidence was being dismembered in the blender of guilt, shame, and familial obligations. For these hidden cherry-suckers, there is going to be a new light of higher awareness shone on them as your 2nd chakra heals. You will release old relationships with friends and family that no longer serve you, that are one-way, sucking away what you offer, without giving you a lifeline, an energy-line in return.

What you need is symbiotic connections. What you need is the love and nurturing that will let you flower and show your beauty in full resplendent glory. And, as you do, your self-confidence grows, your cherries multiply and you begin to let your flowers show their different colors and hues as you explore and display new aspects of your creativity, whether in business, art, music or writing.

For you are a true red-blooded expression of the Creator's joy of life, sensuality and creativity. And as you proceed through the shift and balance out your 2nd chakra, you will become more attuned to your inner cherry tree and let all and sundry see aspects of it.

It is no longer time to hide. It is time to shine. Let yourself bear fruit and express your inner self. And so you grow your emotional body. And so you take a step towards your ascension.

Chapter 3
The Fruits of Transformation

Blueberry—*A Naughty Psychic Adventure*

When you taste a blueberry, a rich, luscious flavor bursts into your mouth, providing thrilling nourishment with a hint of naughtiness. The naughtiness is expressed as the dark indigo color that brushes across your tongue and palate.

And this artist's brush is your creator self's naughtiness which is normally expressed psychically by your 3rd eye. It is naughty on the part of the "normal" world that regards such skills as a bit, shall we say, "crazy".

But for you, there is that delightful sense of exhilaration at having tasted the sweet fruit of anti-oxidative insight which spills across your very being.

We say to you: be proud of your psychic skills. Bite into the indigo magic your soul calls forth with the same insouciant abandon with which you bite into that blueberry.

And when you have had only one blueberry, you want more and more. And so it is my friends that once you have tasted the naughty intoxication of your psychic abilities, you will want more and more.

For you have bitten into a portal to the infinite divine wisdom of the Universe. And there is no going back.

And, just like a blueberry, it is very healthy for you, driving your growth.

Banana—*A Stable, Harmonious Symphony of Growth*

Just as a slip on a banana peel can be disastrous, it is when you remove the peel and find the flesh inside that true stability and balance is found from the fruits of sturdiness.

A banana, when eaten, feels soft and almost squishy to some. But it provides the very stability that the absence of a banana peel on a pavement delivers.

It is a miasma of etheric goodness that travels down your oesophagus and cleans the duodenum and imparts essential nutrients to your blood and your cells. It is not a main star. It is somewhat derided. But a banana provides balance and a stable foundation in your life.

A baby will be inherently drawn to a banana. Its softness, its squishiness somehow appeals to something deep inside this baby.

So, we say to you: let the banana appeal to the foundation of your spiritual self which will arise in your spiritual transformations. It is the base from which you grow. Let the banana, when eaten, provide the base health and balance to your body's various systems. Eat a banana when you need electrolytes, when you feel depleted. Eat bananas when you want the foundation to help you grow and connect with Spirit.

Just as the root chakra provides the base for the crown chakra to connect to the Spiritual world in your etheric body, so the banana, as a fruit, provides a stable base for your ongoing spiritual transformation. Eat and rejoice. For you have a balanced and harmonious approach to your growth. And symphonies are all about balance and harmony.

Let the banana harmonize and stabilize you and sing the symphony of the components of your body to the Universe.

Apple—*A Dear Gift of Balance*

You have heard the phrase: "You are the apple of my eye". This connotes a sense of something very special, very dear.

And, dear ones, an apple a day is a very dear offering that you can make to yourself. For this apple contains so many nutrients that it always finds a way to balance your body with electrolytes and vitamins and enzymes.

And so it is that this fruit helps you balance not only your body, but your mind and your soul. For it is in the vibrations of balance and harmony that you find the stability to grow.

For if you tried to accelerate your spiritual growth without balance, you might find yourself tilting in one direction or another and not really feeling like you are going anywhere, not feeling like you are really achieving anything.

An apple, in its pure goodness and chastity gives you the authority and seniority, through the balance it provides, to claim your path as you best know, as a Creator God.

For every moment of life, including the moment of choice for your next step in your spiritual path, is your own volition, your own creation. And, with balance, you choose the next step with confidence and ease.

And so you maintain your health, your rosy glow. Just like Snowwhite in the fairytale. There is no poison in the apple. It is truly wholesome and nourishing. Like apple pie.

Jump up and leap onto your path of mastery, dear ones, for you are being dear to yourself when you eat an apple a day. You not only keep the doctor away, but you become the doctor yourself, healing yourself and the world as you grow into your multidimensional, higher self.

Plum—*Union of Spirit and Matter*

O mighty emblem of succulent riches! A plum is luscious inside and out. Its exterior purple visage signals a densely charismatic nature that will provide indications of hidden riches. For, when you bite into this purple exterior, you are surprised by the golden fruit inside, with its honeyed yellows and prismatic riches.

You have bitten into the gold ducats of the treasure chest that will alchemize your 3rd dimensional density into a union with your divine self, your Christed self.

As you bite into the purple exterior and yellow gold interior you harmonize the gold of your physical kingly self with the purple divinity of your Christed self.

For, in this harmony, the plum symbolizes for us the union of the physical achievement of being crowned as king with the spiritual attainment of accessing your fully Christed self from higher dimensions.

For this, dear ones, is the direction in which we are all heading. Heaven on earth is our destination. We will not suddenly be transported to an ethereal world, with ethereal bodies, as the Shift occurs.

Instead, we will be playing our parts as physical incarnations of our Christed higher selves. We will embody the yellow gold of the interior of the plum in our exterior visage and maintain the Christed purple self on the inside.

By reversing the polarity in this way we transform what is in nature to be new and exciting.

And we also find that we can switch easily to the higher dimensions, where purple becomes our exterior and yellow gold our brilliant interior.

Bite into a plum to accelerate your ascension with the Shift. And bask in the rays of the golden crown and glory that you will embody as your crystallize into your purple Christed self.

Cherry—*A Saucy, Vivacious Tumble*

It is an ontological truth that a cherry makes you happy. Pop one in your mouth and a delicious red smear of juicy, anti-inflammatory goodness spread across your mouth, like a natural blush of excitement. Pop another, and another, and your scarlet self emerges, a self that is saucy and bold; vivacious and full of mirth.

Dear ones, when you want to pick up your mood from depression, from despondency, eat a few cherries and let the flavor of the divine will and pioneering spirit of the creator course through your veins.

Let the color of the blood match the color of your scarlet-stained mouth. Lick your lips and apply the natural color rouge to your lips. And then send a kiss to yourself with this cherry-lipsticked face. Be saucy, be full of life, and enjoy your moment of scarlet glory.

A cherry's texture is yielding, soft and supple, yet not mushy. So eat the cherry and find ways to express your saucy side in a way that is appealing and alluring. Transform yourself into the sexy coquette who summons all and provides the gaiety for others to frolic in. And smile, part those crimson lips, for life is a dance to be enjoyed.

Watermelon—*The Creator Within*

When you bite into a watermelon, delicious, cool, soothing juice squirts into your mouth and quenches the thirst inside.

The thirst that you always feel, not only for liquid nutrients as provided by fruits and water, but the thirst for your own awakening, your own spiritual thirst to recognize the truth of who you really are.

You are a magnificent being of light who has chosen to come to the Earth plane to play a game within the third dimensional plane. There are parts of your soul and Higher Self in other dimensions and parallel universes. There are many aspects of you that connect together in a web of energy across all the multiverses, across the simplistic notions of time and space.

Because you sense how magnificent you truly are, yet you sense the temporality, the transience of your earthly existence, you thirst for the knowledge, the insight that will reveal to you the juicy flesh of the cut-up watermelon, so that your thirst might finally be quenched, so that you might finally find the nutrients to make you grow, to make you rise up into your higher sense of awareness and being.

Simply believe that this watermelon is inside you. And this is the truth. Peel away and cut through the layers of disbelief, and grief and anger and sadness. Peel away this sense of unmovable limitation, and let your senses reveal to you the red, juicy watermelon underneath.

And admire yourself. And taste yourself. For you see, you are and have always been the very nourishment that you are looking for.

You have all the answers within yourself, for you are connected to the web of light that comprises the heavens, the multiverserses, all the aspects of Creator. For you are an aspect of that Creator.

Cranberry—*Taste Your Dreams*

There is a moment in everyone's life when it seems like there isn't enough time to do what we want to do. We always wanted to learn how to play the guitar, we always wanted to ice skate, we always wanted to go surfing. Yet we never made the time for these fun activities in our lives. We always said: later, we will find time. Yet, later never came.

Some people go through their entire lives waiting for the right time to go forward and explore and check off all the things they hoped they would do one day. And then life passes them by, and they end their lives disappointed.

The point we are trying to make, dear ones is that just like the cranberry adds spice and pizzaz, through its sweetness, to food, to salads, to life, similarly, the adventures that we postpone, that we say we will try another day, add meaning to our lives, for they provide fulfillment through new experiences.

Try a salad both with and without cranberries and taste the difference. Then taste a cranberry muffin or a cranberry pancake and then taste a plain muffin or a plain pancake.

The plain foods will nourish you, just as life can still be lived even if you never live out your dreams. But the taste is insipid and a little restrained. The irony is that those who have never tasted the cranberry pancakes or cranberry muffins continue eating the plain ones, not knowing what they are missing. Similarly, those people who postpone the exciting things in life they desire deep down to pursue, might never know what they are missing until they pass to the other side and see it from their soul's perspective.

Your life, this particular incarnation, never comes back, dear ones. This body, this lifetime, this family, is a unique experience at this moment that will never be recreated. Live in the moment and grab your experiences, live out your dreams. Otherwise you might end your life in regret.

You can add many sweeteners and syrups to plain pancakes and plain muffins. But the taste, while sweet, just as palliatives in life like alcohol and chocolates are distracters, can never approximate the surprising taste and special flavor that the cranberries of life, those special events that are unique and different, can provide.

Live out your dreams dear one. Ask for guidance and support from the Creator. Set the intention and opportunities to live out your dreams will present themselves to you.

Date—*Sweet Sustenance for your Inner Child*

When you don't have a date, eat a date instead. When you feel lost and undernourished in love, eat a date. Enjoy its succulence, enjoy its luscious sweetness. For, in biting into this fruit of the Creator, you connect with that core of sweetness and nourishment that is part of all.

A date is deceptive in its looks. It feels like it can't possibly taste good. Might it be unappetizing? But the best things in life come in wrappers that might be deceptive.

So, when choosing a date, look beyond the outside package. When choosing a lover or a partner for your life, look beyond the outside appearance. Love and nourishment come from the core of the being inside. That is what endures over time, and is ageless.

The outer form can hide much that is in misalignment for you. Take, for example, multicolored candies that children eat. Yes, they are sweet, and they have beautiful wrappers. But they are misleading in their sweetness. For they can corrupt the balance and equilibrium of the endocrine systems of these children.

So, we say to you, be careful who you choose to partner up in your life with. Do not choose based just on the wrapper, and do not be taken and mistaken with artificial sweetness.

For it is the innocent child within you whose balance is being corrupted if you are not careful. It is your very spiritual soul that can find its compass, its sense of direction, lost.

Choose your date and partner carefully, my dears. Nourish that child within you. Dare to eat the pedestrian date and grow the seeds of truly sweet sustenance.

Grapefruit—*Complexity for the Soul*

Just as a star explodes in a supernova, a grapefruit explodes its bitterness onto our palates. It is a monumental surprise. The acidity is expected, but there is an astringent bitterness that throws first tasters off their game. They make a face. They say does anybody really eat this fruit?

We say to you that this initial taste is deceptively misleading. In fact, the second and third times you eat the grapefruit, you will find its flavor deepens and yields harmonies and dissonances that are unexpected, arising in you a complexity of understanding that you might not have been at ease to pursue earlier.

So as you eat more grapefruit, you palate's ability to assimilate complexity grows. And, hence, you are nourished. It is no surprise that grapefruit is one of the healthiest fruits on the planet. It nourishes your body with vitamins and antioxidants. And it nourishes your soul's desire for adventure, for complexity. It appeals to the creator in you that wishes for new ways to express the beauty and magnificence of the Creator.

Eat a grapefruit with a smile, knowing that you are nourishing your soul and your body at the same time. For they are intimately connected, as your spirit well knows.

And just as the acidity in the grapefruit might cause an initial shock, when life's challenges suddenly surprise us, we feel shocked, shaken asunder.

But when we regroup and look at the problem with some distance a second and a third time, it becomes not so insurmountable and we begin to envision and create the solutions that we, as Creator-gods are so adept at.

We express our divinity in our creativity and our complexity.

Guava—*Milk of Life*

A succulent white burst of juicy flavor, a guava defies gravity in its expression of ethereal spirituality.

A guava is green outside yet milky white inside. The milk of life, of heaven is inside this green expression of your inner being. As you bite into the guava, taste the Milky Way to your heart's core, to your soul's essence. And let that sense of complete surrender to this nourishment that is beyond comprehension envelop you, and provide your inner being with a release and a path for forward momentum.

A guava has a crunch to it as well. The crunch is symbolic of the path you are treading, for there is some gravel often on the ground, which seems to shift and move as you tread along. And the crunch is part of your journey, and it is temporary.

For when you bypass the crunch and focus on the juicy fruit cooling your oesophagus and inner body, you find your path is widening and you can see further ahead. And when you turn your head around to look back, you see the progress you have made as a pilgrim in your journey to the soul of your Higher being.

Let the guava cool and nourish your inner being while you progress to your Higher Being. The crunch, dear ones, is not important. The distractions in life are not important. It is your focus on your journey, what your soul came here to do that will fulfill you.

Drink the milk of your passion, of your soul's journey and find yourself well on your way to your destination, which eventually will lead you to the heart of God.

Mango—*Remember your God-Self*

Alfonso is a type of mango. Alfonso is also the name of a king. And, indeed, a mango is a king of fruits because it is so sunny, so regal, so magnificent in its expression of sunshine, glory of self, and celebration of the Creator. Eat a sunny, yellow mango and taste the rich unique taste of your Alfonso, of your kingship, of your divine nature.

As you bite into the juicy flesh of the divine you feel a stirring in your mouth and in your body, of a recognition. The taste is special and different, yet you remember it in your cells. A mango may be exotic, yet it always feels familiar, always feels like it belongs inside your body as you eat it. Dear ones this is because you already taste like and express your divine self, but it has been hidden away from you in veils and shrouds.

As the Shift in Consciousness progresses you will be given many opportunities to reclaim and recognize your divine, regal self.

Eat the mango, eat the Alfonso and rekindle the knowledge of your Sun god self. Let the yellow flames of taste glow within you, providing nourishment to your body, your cells, and your ancient regal wisdom of your Higher Self.

And as you discover more about yourself with you expression of Alfonso, you will find that your path becomes more and more glorious, more and more tasty, like a ripe, luscious mango, ready to be eaten, ready to be devoured, ready to be experienced.

Hearken to your Alfonso, dear ones. The clarion call of your god self calls. Hearken to the call.

Orange—*Willfulness Abated*

Just as an orange is fleshy and juicy, life itself is fleshy and juicy. It might have a tangy acidity at times, which can get sometimes too acerbic, but overall the sense is of a grand experience, one that unfolds naturally, surprisingly and in ways that sometimes bewilder us.

An orange is also a great source of sustenance, of vitamin C, of the orange goodness that keeps our bodies aligned both in a physical way, and also with all that is. So, an orange, like life, is essentially beneficial, but there are times when one feels like one has had enough, like "I have had too much orange juice" today—too many calories, or the desire to taste something different. Perhaps a different juice, like pineapple!

Similarly, as people experience the changes that the Shift brings, they will feel at times that they have had enough of life, that if life is beneficial, if it is full of vitamin C, like an orange, sometimes the lessons are bitter, and the acidity of the taste, of the experience of life, gets to be too much.

We say to them that do not judge your experience but just let it be. The orange can never be an enemy to your body. And your life, as guided by your Higher Self, and your spiritual guides, can never be bad for you. It is all experience. You can learn something from every event in your life. So we say to you that embrace the orange, embrace the acidity, embrace the experience of life.

For if you feel like you have had enough and want to try something else, to move on from this incarnation, the choice is always available to you, but later, from a higher perspective, you might feel regret that you did not express yourself completely, did not nourish yourself completely with the Vitamin C that additional oranges would have provided in the garden of your life.

So we say to you, do not rush, enjoy the experience. This body, this life, these friends, this family, this lover will never take this form again. And you might have regrets if you choose to give up the nourishment of life too fast.

Live in the moment, live in the NOW. Know that you are protected and guided always by the beings of higher dimensions. Know that this orange of life is one you chose to bite into and experience.

Solar Plexus Chakra
Oak Tree—Embodying the 3rd Chakra

Ordinarily, the oak tree is considered to be pedestrian, one that is readily seen all over the world, one that is ubiquitous. And so we use the wood to make oak panels, to make oak furniture, to cover our worlds with a strength and solidity that we need.

And we, as trees of connection between the earth and the spiritual plane, embody the oak tree's solidity and its strength when we express the will of what we want to do through our third chakra, our solar plexus chakra.

And you might say, that yes, I understand the ubiquity of this for, indeed, we all have solar plexus chakras and we all express our will in the world. But what we say to you is that yes, you all have the potential to be solid, to be strong, to be oak-like, but not all of you take up this potential. You neglect, and do not water and nourish, your internal strength. And, so, you leave yourself open to infestation and disease. And, so, your oak tree is no longer strong. And, so, you no longer have the self-confidence to express your will in the world.

Hearken to the inner voice of your 3rd chakra, and you will be able to set a course that is measured and perfect for you. The first thing that you must do is to clear out the infestations, the noises, the insects who want to tear away and suck dry that inner sense of your own encoding and blueprint of spiraling growth that you were born with. You must fumigate yourself, for as you have grown up, you have been encoded by others' visions of your future.

Your parents might have wanted you to be a doctor or a lawyer. Your relationship partner might encourage you to give up your dreams of entrepreneurship and risk, and trade in your dreams, for the dreary everyday reality of a 9-5 job, or even a longer confinement in the artificial office of despair and stagnation.

So we ask you now to imagine a solar sun being birthed in the middle of your stomach. It flames bright and gloriously golden. And as it ignites and glows within your stomach, it begins to purify and burn up the putrefaction that has been perpetrated by others of your inner divine design, your inner divine blueprint of who and what you want to be, of who and what and how you wish to express your will in the world.

And as you begin to release this cultural programming of others from your space, as you begin to not let others define your life and experience in your lifetime, you will also see the physical manifestations of this in your body.

You will no longer slouch as you become more confident. You will no longer get stomach aches or diarrhea when you worry, or have anxiety about the future. You will no longer develop ulcers. You will no longer hesitate to step forward. You will stand up strong and solid and endure the trials that life throws your way. You will know that in your sturdiness you will indeed manifest your inner dream; you will indeed become once again the sturdy oak that has endured all and maintained its integrity.

And so we ask you now to claim your inner Sun, to become the Jupiter of old, ignite your oak tree that has been harvested and anchors your 3rd chakra of will, of manifestation, of how you express yourself in the material world. Set the intention that you will claim the wealth and abundance that is your birthright, that you will stay healthy, that you will enjoy the ride, and play the game of life with happiness and with a smile.

And as you do this people will be attracted to you and they will ask for your advice and for your help. For everyone would like a piece of strong and sturdy oak within the foundation of their lives.

Chapter 4
Colors for Growth

Olive Green—*Ontological Joie de Vivre*

Incidental though it might seem, the shade of olive, a kind of darker green, indicates shade, Mediterranean breezes and delight, as conveyed in the healthy, delicious properties of the olive itself.

Olive suggests health, beauty, sensuality. Whenever the Europeans referred to Italians or Spanish people of a slightly darker hue, since ancient times, they referred to them as olive-skinned. There was and still is a sense that the olive nature is one of serenity, of an unabashed letting go, of a *joie de vivre*.

And it is this *joie de vivre*, this sense of letting go that we wish to inculcate in you, dear one.

Let yourself bite into an etheric, glowing olive in front of you. As you do, the color olive spills across your mouth, flowing down your digestive system, through your body, enlightening all of your cells with that awareness of Mediterranean bliss, the pleasure of sunlight, azure breezes, calm and fiery siestas. Let yourself now be washed away into a world of sensuous abandon where you agree to taste life, taste food, taste sex and enjoy your body without any guilt.

For you have been told so often, as a child, that you should respect boundaries, that you should behave yourself, that you should not behave in a way that is shameful. Control of you by others has been programmed in you since you were born.

Find yourself now lying naked on a beach, stretched out on Mediterranean sands, allowing the sun of ease and protection and permission to wash all over you. A human of your choice, naked and sexual, fulfilling all your fantasies, walks up to you. There is a sense of urgency, of passion, of expression of a merging of your bodily forms. This human opens a vial of olive cream, and begins to rub it slowly over your body in a range of motion that is sensual, enlightening, awakening, giving permission to the senses to be, allowing your *joie de vivre* to become your destiny.

Awaken, dear ones to an enjoyment of every moment of your life. Enjoy your body, enjoy your food, enjoy exercise, enjoy communion with others. Move yourself and feel the sensation of every atom in motion. And you will find yourself becoming increasingly Mediterranean, increasingly sensual, and increasingly open, letting go of cultural programming that is meant to inhibit you.

Rest and breathe out your olive breath, rekindle your body and let it burn up in an olive green sense of completeness. You have just taken another step on your journey home.

Brown—*Murky Happenstance Overcome*

Nowhere is it said that one must obey one's parents. Well, perhaps the Bible and Koran and Talmud say so. But is this really a truth that must always be upheld? Or is it part of a culture that wants to make sure that people's opinions conform to orthodoxy?

What we must get you to recognize is that it is all right to let go of religious doctrine that is counter-intuitive or not in your best interest. So, if you have a drunk lush as a parent, who asks you to keep imbibing alcohol with them, and you are an adolescent who is scared, it is ok to not listen to this parent, and to seek help.

At times like this, when all is falling apart, when you are torn between the desire to listen to a parent, who supposedly knows more, and your inner knowledge that tells you that you cannot do so for your own sanity, then you are in a world of brown, a world of shit, if we could use that word.

Know that the objective here is not to confound you but to let you know that there are states of awareness on this planet, when you are thrust into a murky emotional state, when nothing seems to make sense. Yet this state is an important catalyst for growth. For it is when your back is against the wall, it is when things are most foul and not fair, that you begin to really question orthodoxy, and start wondering whether your inner knowledge might not hold more truth, more light, more ascended mastery.

So when you begin to shine your inner light, your inner wisdom, into a world of murky browns, you begin to wash away the shit, to let it go back to where it came from. And even if the parent is upset with you or makes threats against you, you must ignore it and believe in yourself. Let your white light of purity blot out the brown leaves of decay and stagnation that others throw at you.

For it is not compost that you need, it is not dross from a drugged out or drunk or maladjusted parent. What you need is love, what you need is compassion. And when you can offer these to others, even when they do not give it to you, is when you become part of an ascended mastery, teaching the browns of the world to wash themselves properly and become part of the light.

For you have become a teacher to your parent.

Emerald Green—*Gleaming, Gloaming Through Life*

If you try to ponder the meaning of life, you will find yourself wallowing in a mystery that is unknowable. Life is part of a stream of everything that has no beginning and no end. And so, in trying to understand infinity, you can tie yourself up in knots, so to speak.

So break away from the larger picture and try to focus in on your immediate issues that are in front of you. Imagine a beautiful emerald green wand in front of you that is your expression of healing, of beauty, of growth, and of solutions to that which is bothering you.

Hold this etheric wand in your right hand and feel the emerald green energy beginning to flow through your hand, through your wrists and arms, up to you body and here it starts spreading all over, like a miasma of optimism and shining brilliance.

You feel coated and gloated in this gloaming, magical emerald green of Source that, like the Emerald green city in Oz, is a beacon to that other, mystical self that can solve all and seduce the senses with fun along the way.

As your body vibrates now with the frequency of emerald green, your higher mind turns on and allows you to see your immediate life from a detached perspective. Visualize now this bright emerald stone gleaming and gloaming in your higher mind, connecting you with the insights and solutions to all that which bothers you and worries you right now.

Close your eyes and take a deep breath. See this emerald in your higher mind now beaming emerald green light into your heart, and let it glow, in a beautiful emerald gloaming.

Now focus on the one problem that is bothering you, place your emerald wand on your gloaming emerald heart and let your heart whisper to you the answer as to how you should proceed on the next step.

And know, dear one, even if it seems like the answer is still not clear, the Universe will provide you with the dewy, emerald signs to light your path through the gloaming, into the gleaming Emerald city of your dreams.

Magenta—*Conductor of Your Magical Soul*

Ordinarily when a piece of magenta cloth is placed on top of one's third eye, on that space between one's forehead, where more than you can imagine can be accessed, one feels a sense of displacement, as if one is being called to enter into a vortex of color, of psychedelia, of an alternate world.

And indeed, dear ones, magenta is a color of magic, of the mage in the making who wishes to transcend the boundaries of everyday reality and find the true meaning, the true existence and consequence of all there is.

And so, this color, whether it is a physical piece of cloth that you place on your forehead, or simply a visualization of a magenta beam of light entering your third eye, will give you permission to turn on your inner mage, your inner magician, your inner sorcerer.

Use these energies lightly, dear one, for in going too fast you might get scared at what you see, and also in going too fast, you might, in your new awareness, wonder: "What am I doing on Earth when all is so beautiful elsewhere. I want to be there. I don't want to be here." And so we say, use the magenta vibration in small doses, to awaken in you your sense of your inner powers, but be prudent in your use.

And in your prudence, your inner magician will flourish like a conducter finally being given a chance to command all the musicians, all the energies of the Universe to create, to transform, to perform magic.

And, indeed, magic is like music, in that it works with vibration, with specific tones and thoughts. And the magenta overlay, your conductor-self, not only directs all the other pieces, but also is a conductor from higher awareness of the specific instructions on how to proceed, on how to organize the magical within the earthly plane.

Arise, dear ones, to your inner magician. Let the magenta cloth, the mangenta ray of light, penetrate those veils of ignorance and place the conductor's baton in your hand once again. For you are about to reclaim your mastery as a being of immense light and love, conducting this light to others and creating a symphony of transformation, directed by your magical energies.

Say aloud to yourself: "I am a being that is masterful and grand. I am a magician of immense power. And I am a conductor for the Creator to be of service and awaken others to the Shift in consciousness that is at hand. Let's all play our instruments, our vibrations together and create a new symphony as we all ascend to higher vibrations, to a new Earth filled with new potentials and new magical deities: ourselves."

And so it is.

Aquamarine—*Folding Into Your Divine Self*

Not once, but twice, three times you want to yell out loud: "What is the meaning of it all? Why is life so difficult." Why can't it all be sun and caviar and champagne?

And this is a valid complaint. Indeed, there do exist planets and places in the Universe where life is just so: sun and caviar and champagne. But then it wouldn't be Earth, it wouldn't be the place you have come to learn a lesson, to grow, to expand and to become the higher consciousness that you were always destined to be.

Imagine, if you will, the color aquamarine shooting out of your sixth chakra, its mix of green and blue melding into a cooling, icy vibration which allows you to let go of the heated emotions that keep you chained to the fears and worries of the third dimension, of this game that we are all playing.

Feel the cooling, wafty breeze of this color spilling out into your aura, cooling, embalming, embracing that which needs to be transmuted to a higher perspective. And as this color emerges and spills out of your 3rd eye, it is in its very source of the 3rd eye, the higher dimensional perspective, that the perspective and information stored in your aura can change, can be released, can be cooled down to a more etheric vibration.

So take a deep breath and feel the cooling, wafty breeze of the Creator. Imagine an azure, aquamarine horizon across the beach as you stare at the ocean's edge. Feel your connection, through the aquamarine mist to all that is. And, as you do, this aquamarine color spills from the sky into the ocean water, turning it into a shade of aquamarine, or higher consciousness.

And, now, you, standing on the beach, already finding the aquamarine vibration spilling from your Higher Self into your aura, find a match between your inner divine self and the outer divine reality spilling out of the horizon.

You jump into the waters, aquamarine says hello to aquamarine. You are now part of the ocean of all there is, the building blocks of higher consciousness. Meld in and float and flow. For you are as divine as the horizon. You have always been divine. You will always be divine. You are god incarnate. Flow and embrace your aquamarine, universal self. Connect with you inner God.

And breath in aquamarine prana from the air, from the water and replenish the never-ending source of vitality, of growth that is you.

And that is why you came to Earth, and this is why you chose to play in this game, to grow, to expand to have the experience of an inner aquamarine finding a match in the divine aquamarine that has always been there and always will.

Rust Orange—*Galvanized Beacons of Light*

If you try to say hello to someone and they ignore you, or treat you contemptuously, you often feel crestfallen. You feel that you have tried to reach out, you have tried to express your friendliness and your love, but it has been cast aside, it had been tossed into the dust and dirt of that which is useless, unneeded, or simply, garbage.

And from this dust bowl of garbage that your love and friendliness has been tossed into, you start to dissolve into a small cone of disappointment. You let the sharp acidity of those who have spurned you affect your metallic integrity, your clear connection to source, your elemental connection to source, and in the curdling of your dreams, you slowly begin to rust. And as the acidic waters of desolation take their toll, you lose your sparkle, you lose your luster, as you become part of a rust bowl.

But love and happiness, dear ones, can never come forth from disuse, from being allowed to rust, from being allowed to burnish[11]. For in the rusting lies irreparable corrosion, that is very hard to recover from, as you enter into a spiral of not trusting others anymore, of not giving of your love and happiness anymore, and thus you are spurned even more, and you rust even more.

What you need, dear ones, is a true friend, one who will always be there for you, one who will never let you rust, one who will transform the rusty orange coat you have accepted for yourself into a glowing, sparkling more assiduously bright orange of emotional connection, a higher vibration of family.

And this is when you call in your true friends, dear ones, your soul family, who have travelled with you from the higher dimensions, who vibrate at your frequency, who are constant in their attentions, for they know instinctively who you are, and they are attracted to you.

They might live across the four corners of the globe, they might never even have met you physically, but they will hear your clarion call for succor and redress to stop the rusting, to galvanize you to mightier strength and perpetual industry.

So see yourself now sending out a sparkling, gleaming orange light from your second chakra out into the world, out into the ethers. Set your intention that this ray of light find out those true friends, those soul sparks of yourself, both incarnate and on the other side of the veil that are available to help you alight, burn more brightly and galvanize in strength.

And as you set this intention, you will see the orange ray of light spinning out in multiple threads and strands, weaving an exquisite pattern of connection and searching that is specific for you, and for the coordinates and location of your soul family. And you will suddenly feel a jolt as these filaments start connecting with the true friends, the true soul elements of yourself. You do not need to visualize them. Instead, you will suddenly feel the electricity coming back through the woven pattern, back through the many, myriad filaments, burning bright, with the tigers of love and burning love, igniting your 2nd chakra with fire, burnishing and galvanizing it into life and longevity.

And as you accept this unconditional love coming your way from so many different sources of love, both on this Earth plane and from your many guides and aspects of the soul family across the Universe, you breathe in with gusto and pride that sense of self-glory and orange, rust-free brightness. For you have been restored to life and are galvanized to action.

You step forth again, proffering your love and friendliness to all asunder. And if they still spurn you occasionally, you simply smile in your strength and confidence and compassionately wish them well.

In your strength of higher and unconditional love you move from the rust bowl of disuse to a galvanized beacon of glowing love that through its strength allows others to be and in that compassionate acceptance hearkens in them, eventually, more love and acceptance in their hearts, if they so wish.

Pray to the Creator and be in the glory of who you are and love unconditionally. And hence you will live your life in a galvanized way.

Cobalt Blue—*Mine Your Life Into a Beauteous Expression of Your Destiny*

Inside a cobalt mine, it is dark, it is dank, it is a bit disconcerting. So when the cobalt is uncovered, when its shocking blue face appears in front of the visage of the miner, it is, in a sense a miasma, a mirage of everything beautiful, serene and free. Everything outside the mine.

And so, dear one, when you mine through the dark tunnels of your life, when it seems like it is all toil and despair, know that within the darkness, the dear, electric cobalt blue of adventure, of pristine beauty, can suddenly appear, out of the blue.

And in this very blueness, you will find the certainty for your path, the certainty that validates all the struggles before and makes them worthwhile. And as you put down your tools, as you contemplate the beauty of the blue rock within the black façade, you will know that life, like nature, has many gems hidden in unknown and unforeseen places.

And you can use this blue cobalt now, just like the porcelain makers of old, to create a new tapestry of expression, of delight, of excitement. Choose your next project, choose your next step in life and create a beautiful container to help it manifest as you desire. Now use the cobalt blue of your endeavors, of your hard work, to start painting and creating that which you are about to express as your next step. Beautify and make it pretty. Add the emblems that represent you, and all the difficulties you have had to go through to reach the place that you are at now. And smile, for your creation, your expression is one of a kind, is a kind of cobbled ice cream of blue confidence piercing the dark mysteries of life and of your journey.

And as others see what you have created, they will notice your cobaltian blue of certainty and of beauty. They will know that in your confidence, you have found a way to project your energies into the world, so that they will be beneficial to all. And even if it is just to notice your cobalt blue beauty, even if it is just to commend your ability to discover such a beautiful color as a reward for your searching work in the tunnel of your life, know that the people who notice will not forget. You will leave an imprint on their souls for all eternity. And so you succeed in finding a new expression for the being that is you, a new way of impacting others, a new way of carving out your Akashic record for posterity.

Astounding and beautiful. That is who you are in your potter's, creator's cobalt blue expression. Embrace it and celebrate it.

And continue to dig deep into the tunnel of your life, dear one, for who knows what other gem, what other new color that allows you to express yourself in a new way, is around the corner.

Tan—*From Fossil to Cosmic Being*

In the event that things don't work out the way you want them to, in the event that life hurtles you down the corridor of no return, find a way to step on the brake, find a way to pull out the stops, for you are in control and you can take the reins.

Within the tannic inhibitions of your metallic life, you might feel as if you are being burned and treated, tanned like a piece of leather into something that is like a dinosaur, dead yet still living in a sort of ghoulish way, beaten down, yet still around, still moving, still serving a function.

When you find yourself tanned out by life into a form that is not where you wish to be, find a new way to be tanned, find a new way to take control of your life, to drive yourself to your next destination in a positive, controlled way.

Seek out the sunshine that is filtering in through nature. Let it enter your body; let it tan your skin. Bathe in this natural light of the cosmic father of all there is. Let your cells be infiltrated by a natural, cosmic beauty and reality.

And so you transform yourself from an artificially treated tanned being to one that is naturally tanned by the Creator, to arise and awake in you your natural sensibilities, your natural talents, your natural purpose in life, what we would like to call your destiny.

You now find a way to reassess where circumstances have been taking you. You now find a way to reexamine the people, the situations, the circumstances that had allowed you to be the recipient of others' treatments, the artificial tanning to the fossilization of your life.

And in doing so, now, in claiming your own natural tan, you, the person, the master, the son of the Sun, or the daughter of the Goddess, for both indeed are aspects of the same, now claim the divinity within you to take a step towards a future you wish to create, a future that is *brulante* and smoky, yet silky and smooth.

For a natural tan, dear one, imparts a glow of health, of radiance, a burning desire to experience life in all its aspects and dimensions. And you look like a ripe apple, with reddish cheeks, which match the tan of knowledge, of cosmic undertaking and of wisdom. And keep seeking the sun, the cosmic energies of the Universe, dear one, for as you know, tans have a tendency to wear off under the clouds.

Embrace and reconcile a natural existence with the Earth that you live on. And in so doing you find yourself regenerating every cell of your body, so that the fossilized dinosaur from the past is now reborn as an entirely new being that is light, airy, multidimensional and part of the fabric of all that is.

Indigo—*Return to the Source of Certainty and Co-Creation*

Assume that life will take you where you need to go. Assume that everything always plays out the way it is meant to. Assume that your future will be created by you as a co-creation with Spirit and with your Higher Self, and you will find yourself in a vibration of confidence, of ease, of allowing. You will find yourself vibrating as an Indigo.

And it is no coincidence, dear ones, that the new, talented and gifted young ones who are entering the Earth plane to help the evolution of humanity, and many of whom are Avatars from the far reaches of this Universe and from other Universes, are called Indigo children. They are indigo in their certainty, in their wisdom, and in their tenacity for facing the hurdles that life throws their way in this 3rd dimensional game of duality called Earth.

If you find yourself spinning away from certainty, drowning in tears of sorrow and desolation, and wondering where exactly your future will take you; if you find yourself reacting to the dramatic and mostly unexpected changes coming to the Earth over the next few years, which will indeed come, as they are part of the ongoing Shift in Consciousness, that is when you must decide how to wean yourself back to an indigo state and reclaim and reconnect with your Higher Self, your higher levels of awareness that will see you through uncertainty and doubt and desolation.

One of the ways you can do this, dear ones, is to find yourself happily rejoicing in the beauty of that which is unspoiled and unmarred by humanity's duality and fears. Seek out the babies in their carriages who smile at you for no reason and beam the unconditional love of the Creator at you through their eyes. Commune with the stars out on a rock, on a mountaintop, and sing the praises of love and of beauty as you find yourself sinking into the earth and towering up to the sky at the same time.

For you are earth and sky. You are sun and moon. You are yin and yang. You are part of infinity and you are also a specific flavor and expression of this infinity that cannot be replicated, that cannot be duplicated, that cannot be domesticated.

And once you rediscover that unconditional love and sense of group identity that is the norm in the higher dimensions, you automatically start pulling in the indigo light of certain belief, of co-creative energy and fantastic futures full of abundance, creativity and multitude.

For you are a being of light and as you tune into the indigo light you find your sense of self expanding, and you find that you have more abilities than you ever imagined, and you find that you are the creator of your destiny. You find yourself to be God.

And, so, you step forward with alacrity on your next step, knowing that things are not just happening to you, knowing that life is a game to be played, a play to be acted, a song to be sung, joyously, ceremoniously and ultimately in reverence. Reverence for your particular expression of the Creator in your soul, and reverence for all there is. And an indigo you automatically are.

Lime Green—*Astringent Cleanser of Wounding*

Ordinarily one would say that lime green is not a very soothing color, that there is something finicky in its very lime-ness, in its very implied acidity. The word lime itself connotes a sense of tartness, of being not so easily accessible in large quantities. And then there is the color itself, a pale shade of green, a pastel-like copy of something that should perhaps be richer.

These thoughts, dear ones, are those that might confound you and represent the intellectual, thinking aspect of you that has been programmed to over-think and intellectualize that which should be simple, accepting and loving. Lime green is a shade of the Creator that is perfect in its tone, in its flavor, in its tartness.

When you are feeling down about a certain event in your life, when your family or friends try and pull you down, use lime green to purify and cleanse. First use first aid on yourself. Over the wounds that have been opened and skewered by the put-downs and pull-downs of family members, of trusted friends, add a little bit of lime green.

See it being poured from a first aid bottle as a lime green liquid into your gaping wounds, asking for succor and relief. And as the green comes in, there might be a slight initial sting, a tartness, as in any good astringent, but then there will come a sense of dissipation of the hurt and wounding that has pierced your inner armor.

Now you are ready, dear one, to fill an etheric aerosol can with this beauteous lime green cleaner from the Creator. Go ahead now and spray the space around you. Spray the relatives and friends who keep crossing the line with you. Deodorize and defang them with the lemony lime green astringent and cleanser that the Creator has provided you. And start feeling fresh again. Start feeling like nothing can harm or pierce your emotional armor anymore. And wear you Creator's body-suit with pride, knowing that the warrior within you has learnt to defend him or herself again with a certain panache and color that was unexpected, perhaps a little astringent, but very effective.

Know that lime green, that antiseptic of the Creator, is available for you for first aid whenever you need it. But you can always use it in small quantities every few days to just release and cleanse any unwanted energies that might have crept into your space without you noticing. And, so, sing a hymn of thankfulness to the Creator and sprinkle a little lime green spray on the Earth, on this globe, for we could all use some disinfectant, we could all use some first aid for the many troubles and wounding that we have suffered in this experiment, in this Earthly game.

And as you are opened up to your divine nature more and more by the coming Shift, you will be able to forgive others with compassion from your higher perspective, as you grow to realize more and more that the wounding and hurting was meant to occur, was part of the game, for that is how spiritual growth occurs very quickly. That is how you grow to connect back with the Avatar that you are in other dimensions.

Forgive, forget, cleanse and deodorize that which has stuck to you, that which is earthly, that which is third-dimensional. New vistas and new horizons await you. And lime green is a tool, a bridge to cleanse, that will help get you there.

Fuchsia—*Remembering the Particles of Higher Intelligence*

Certainly, when one observes the brightness and vividness of the color fuchsia, there is an immediate sense of shock, of being shaken up to a starker, more brightly observed mood.

It is almost as if someone has put a spotlight directly aimed at your eyes, at your brain, at your inner soul. For, in this brilliant pinkish-violet light of the creator, stands the merging of the love and transmutative abilities of your path in life. As you begin to step forward and change and grow into higher aspects of yourself, you find that there are pieces of you that begin to take on a fuchsia color. As they are transformed by the love that you are becoming, they begin to glow in a fuchsian way, transmuting any old patterns, any old karma that you might have carried around you for a long time.

Of course, dear ones, you can make this into a more intentional practice, to accelerate your growth, your momentum into the New Age of spiritual awareness.

Imagine if you will, a huge fuchsia spotlight beaming down from the heavens into your crown chakra. As this light hits your pineal gland, it starts releasing stem cells of fuchsia brightness that flit and float and start igniting parts of your right brain that had previously been turned off, had previously been on a dormant mode, while you went through this game of karma on the 3rd dimension. And as these cells wake up now, in your right brain, they allow you to raise your perception, raise your consciousness and review your life from a more enhanced perspective.

Visualize yourself seeing these fuchsia particles of your right brain lighting up, and then see some of the veils that had kept your right brain from coming alive beginning to dissolve. Smile, dear one, for you are beginning to reinvent your god-self. You are beginning to recreate that aspect of you that created this game, this experience.

And now send some of these fuchsian-ignited particles of light down to other parts of your body, to other chakras, commanding them to go where it is most appropriate to heal you for your highest good. And you will see the lights flitting and floating as small particles of light to different nooks and crannies in your physical and etheric bodies. And then let these smart particles of consciousness do their work, alighting you anew to the God being that you are rapidly becoming.

Enjoy a fantastic future now as you begin to create the adventure of your life anew.

Lemon-Lime—*Express Your Fizzy, Effervescent Self with Confidence*

If you like fizzy drinks that pep you up in the summertime, you will enjoy the refreshing taste of lemon-lime soda, slaking down your throat with ease, releasing any built-up lime that has been holding back any expression of yourself, and scenting it in return with a lime scent that is fresh and inviting, squeezing the lemon on top for taste and for juiciness.

And as you feel this fizzy drink slide down your throat, opening and clearing your throat chakra, you envision the color that this drink represents, a lemon-lime mix of green-yellow balancing that bursts forth from your throat chakra, spilling out in spiraling fashion around your body, around your aura.

And as this color of love and of confident expression fills both your throat chakra and your aura and infiltrates your body, you know that you are being healed, being allowed to reclaim that part of yourself that you might have cut off for fear that it would not be allowed to be love, would not be allowed to express itself confidently.

And so your body, you throat, and your aura start vibrating effervescently, bubbling and fizzing in clear alacrity, happy to be allowed be the being of light you were always meant to be. The lemony scent of your etheric being cleanses the wound, the lime is dissolved, and a new lime of mojito tartness and freshness replaces the ancient wounds of yore.

Squeal in delight and make ancient sounds and modern and lemony-limy sounds of delight, for you are an ancient, well-traveled soul who originally came to this planet to have an adventure, to explore the different expressions of self in a 3rd dimensional game of duality. And, as this game has played out, sometimes, you have been allowed to believe that you should not express yourself. You have allowed yourself to hold judgments in your space that restrict you, confine you, and create a cake of lime that blocks you.

And this is all ok, dear one, for this was part of the experience that you originally signed up for. But now, that this game is ending and we are moving to a 4th and 5th dimensional earth, the lemon-lime color of higher love and confident soul expression will very easily release that which has held you back, that which has caked over you, that which has held a yoke over your self-expression.

Squeal again in delight, dear one, for you are an angel of fizzy love and effervescent beauty that can not only be allowed to, but should be proud to, spread your fresh, refreshing lemon-lime taste to all who are open to you. You can only aid, only cleanse, only repair, for your expression is pure love, pure harmony, pure delicacy.

And for those who say to you, shut up, for I do not like fizzy, I do not like lemon-lime, say to them that is ok, I know that we are all attracted to different flavors. But I am proud of my lemon-lime flavor and I will express it confidently, with love and if you do not like it, I would ask you to move to another room, find another being to converse with.

For, I AM who I AM.

Heart Chakra
Willow Tree—Weeping and Loving All So Deeply

Upon learning about the loss of a dear love, one wants to weep. One wants to simply run after them, find them, track them down, and convince them that all is all right. That things will work out. Or if they have passed away, you wonder if that kind of love will ever find its way to you again. Will what you had ever be replaced, and even if it was replaced could it ever really replace the perfection that you encountered before? And so you weep, dripping tears of sadness and abandon from deep with the core of your heart, from where you express your love.

And as you uncover and decode the hurting of loss and cogitate about the next step, your tears create a pattern, a weave of droopiness that is dewy and sprightly, sending waves of gloom across your very core. And, like a weeping willow tree, you send out drooping tentacles of being from the broken heart of your heart chakra, imagining within your tears, the illusion that what was lost was indeed perfect, was indeed a one-time experience, believing, mistakenly that love takes only one particular form.

And so, you express the singularity of a look of unhappiness, of being unrequited, of being simply dissatisfied with life.

But it is within the very droopiness of your weeping willow that you will ultimately find the strength to rekindle yourself. For as you worry about unrequited love and weep, and resonate with all the hurts and travails that have come your way and hurt your heart over your lifetime, you wonder about things and you droop and shed tears.

And the tears you shed have their own innate beauty, for in expressing true emotion you connect with aspects of your Higher Self that live within your sacred heart, that chamber of connection to your god-self that exists within the beauty of the willow tree of your heart chakra.

For it is in finding the beauty in every experience, even the experience of loss, that you will uncover the true meaning of sorrow. You will discover that sorrow is an emotion that can be debilitating and thrust you into fear, if it is allowed to go unchecked for too long. You will discover that indeed fear is a debilitating state, one that arrests all movement, thrusting you into a quagmire of indecision.

But it is in discovering the beauty of who you really are inside, that beautiful person capable of expressing the unconditional love of the Creator in all different types of relationships, that you turn inside-out the weeping of your willow tree into a beauty of repose, as you find that unbounded love within that can always heal the self and others, extending joyous bounty and joyous expressions of beauty and love to all.

And so you transform yourself from a stupor into practical action. You heal your wounds and then you surround yourself with friends and relatives, and, when you are ready, a new lover who will love you for the new you that you are and have become. And you find inner strength in the love that resides in your sacred heart. You find that your willow wood is medicinal, a source for aspirin[12], known since ancient times to cure the sick, to heal the broken heart. For you have always had the means to heal yourself within. You have always been god-like inside and full of boundless love.

And that is why the Persians referred to the willow's love as madness, the mad lover[13]. For it is madness to weep, and it is in the madness of being and embodying unconditional love that you realize that everyone is connected to you, that you are part of all, and hence you love all, because you love yourself.

Your love is one that encompasses the whole Earth. And so you become a planet-wide willow, spreading mad, intoxicated love to all. And you become a Romeo once again, seeking and finding a Juliet in all.

Chapter 5
Flowering Into the Perfumes of Self-Awareness

Rose—*Primal "Rosa" Red of Source*

Smell the high vibrational energy of the rose and you will be transported to higher dimensions, alternative universes and multidimensional realities.

It almost seems like you are entering through the furled leaves into the core of "rosa", of something infinite, beautiful, ephemeral[14].

When you dive into the heart of this rose you enter into the heart of your being, your sacred heart, the love that you are.

So see yourself now jumping into the rose of the color of your choice. See yourself immersed in a sea of perfume and silk and swaddled finery.

And you emerge now in the center of your sacred heart, inside your heart chakra, ready to commune with one, with all, with the Universe.

The rose's energy is that which is the closest to the Creator in this earthly plane. When you smell the rose you connect to that part of yourself that is God.

Imagine four roses—one behind, one in front, one to the east and one to the west of you. Give them multiple colors or the same color if you like.

Create lines intersecting the rose in front to the rose at the back, and a line connecting the rose on the east to the rose on the west.

And you will find yourself in the center of the energies of the cross, the Christ consciousness.

Merge and commune with the Universe through the rose.

Primrose—*Pale Harbinger of Spiritual Awakening*

A pale yellow voice of emerging spring, a primrose is a beacon of the future, of the possibilities that exist.

Its thistle[15] is an inviting surrender to the primal self that wants to break free of the shackles of doomed and gloomy winter.

Pick a primrose from a wild garden and inhale its sweet smell of fantastic abandon and mystical union with pale visions of future glory.

For, as the spring progresses, and more flowers bloom in your heart, with stronger and deeper colors of abandon and glory, you will remember this first one, the pale yet important harbinger of your future growth and unfurling.

For like a flag that is a little worn in its outer layer, as it unfolds, it shows it true deep colors.

So, as your life unfolds in the spring of your spiritual awakening, your pale primrose beauty will unfurl and grow and deepen.

And your flag has its own special signature and emblem. Your primrose of your initiation for growth is your very own unique vibration and smell.

Relish it and celebrate your incipient beauty.

Foxglove—*Fitting into the Shroud*[16]

Within a few weeks of the onset of a terminal disease, a sense of frustration sets in, both amongst those diagnosed, and those trying to cure, doctors and family.

Much is attempted, much is wrung, much is wrought, yet there seems to be no stopping the untethered march to the next level of existence, if there is one, they wonder, after death.

And for the one who has been diagnosed, for the one who now must look mortality in the face, there is much opportunity for spiritual growth, for alignment with the meaning of what they have achieved so far in life, and how they can bring their flowing, weaving threads of everyday existence to a completion.

Much like a foxglove flower that in its grace and beauty fits the digitalis, the human finger, like a glove, spreading in its purple light and color a transmuting energy to transform the travails and horrors of the past into the new light of unconditional love and surrender, the terminally diagnosed human, sees death's shroud, approaching from afar, in the twilight, it's somber shades of dark purple looking to perfectly fit the body of the soon to be deceased.

And will it, the terminally ill one considers, finally allow me to understand all the details and travails of my life that did not make sense? Will it truly take me afar to a new place, a new heaven, a new dispensation?

As soon as the dying one considers this thought, he attracts to him the spiritual beings in the higher dimensions who are his guides and who are waiting to show him the beauty and grace and unconditional love that live on the other side of the veil.

They pop through the approaching purple shroud, showing the colorful stamens of connection to unconditional love that they are, providing the bridge to the expansive part of the self that is much larger than the small piece that came in for this earthly game, in this particular incarnation.

And just as if the soon-to-depart one were to smell the foxglove in his hand, the stamens sending forth luscious waves of cellular love and light in their smell, the guides shine thoughts and images in this one's head, highlighting all the wonderful experiences he has had, reminding him of all those he has helped, all those who have in some way grown by him living his life and being his unique self.

And they also highlight the dark, disappointing times that played out every now and then, those times when fear and terror and disappointment gripped us, conveying us to harshness, drink and perhaps other narcotics.

And they tell the dying man that even those experiences were worthwhile, for every experience allows the soul to grow. And that as he goes through the veil, he will join them in an expanded body that looks down on this game and understands this perspective. They tell him that he will laugh and cry and enjoy every aspect of his life as he reviews it later, and will be eager to try again, either here on Earth or another planet.

For life is an adventure to be lived. Life is an inextinguishable flame of the soul, one that is eternal.

And just because this particular body is soon to be shrouded, this does not mean that the smell of unconditional love will not help this soul to soon find another link, another thread to another life, to another incarnation, to another expression of self that is unique and will allow for more growth, more expansion.

So hug the terminally ill one and send him on his way with love. Do not fret, do not try too hard to save what is already shrouded, what is already moving on. Let it depart in joy and well-loved, reminding the soul inside that this is just a way-station in the larger journey of evolutions.

And so it is.

Hibiscus—*Kneel to Your Inner Soul*

When you are feeling down physically,
When you are about to let yourself reel
Into a marsh of loneliness and theatricality,
That is the time to turn yourself to feel
The inner light, the inner glory
Which shines through you, as you kneel.

For, as you kneel and search for truth,
For guidance, and for your inner sanctity,
You find yourself bowing to soothe
Your perceived god, in ordained piety.
But your perception is not precise, but uncouth;
For it is to yourself you kneel, the inner Almighty.

There was once a time that the hibiscus flower
Was offered up to Ganesh[17] for blessings.
It was a symbol of purity and beauty, a shower
Of heavenly delight, of unleavened setting.
It was sent to find and bring from afar
The golden light of God, the golden netting.

Instead, we now focus on the hibiscus genus
As a source of Ayurvedic treatment,
Using the teas and balms and other means
To soothe ourselves, improve comportment.
For we are learning to offer the dreams
Of a better life, of a better establishment

To ourselves, with love; not seeking succor
And redress outside by kneeling, or offering *puja*[18];
Not limiting ourselves to an outside redeemer,

But finding instead that, by nourishing our inner *raja*,[19]
We discover the deity within. For the true lover
Is your eternal soul, releasing any external Major.

Rhododendron—*Portal to Multidimensionality*

O vast and mighty emblem of the Creator:
You express your beauty in ways that are infinite;
Your flowers are of every different color and every different vibration
Of the Universe[20].

You are the infinity point from which all Creation grows;
You are the balsamic vinegar in a salad,
The zest of life, of a meal, of sustenance,
Of growth.

O Rhododendron of wondrous beauty,
Fire my loins with your sweet smell of piety;
Let my inner core burst and flower in myriad forms
And colors.

Let me express my many facets and dimensions
Like you do, with the colors of the rainbow;
And the infinite variations
Of these colors

Sunflower—*A Shower of Limitless Light*

A sweet nothing whispers in your ear;
Hearken to the lustful desire so near.

As you ascertain and restrain that which
Wants to flow, wants to be heard, near and far,
We ask that you change your focus to a wish;
A wish to let yourself unfurl as a star.

It is as a star you came from afar,
And it is as a star you will bestir, untar.

The Sun is your closest star to observe
Its glowing sense of hot, intense love
Amuses you, yet also lets you bloom in reserve;
For you are about to let loose above.

It is in your bodily expression of sensuality
That you find a true representation of this reality.

Let the chameleon inside you arise and curl;
Let the kundalini uncover your inner flower,
As you move towards the heat of the sun and unfurl,
Allowing that inner heat to explode as a meteoric shower.

Let no one lead you astray or afar;
Become the sunflower that you are.

Poppy—*Billow into Your Dreams*

A poppy billows in the wind, in reds and purples.
Its singular stem expresses a joy and love
For all that is in this world,
To help us overcome unforeseen hurdles.

Pick a purple poppy from the etheric field
Of light and love, and smell its
Delicious perfume of frankincense
And myrrh, of God's glory to which it kneeled.

O poppy of that delicious slumber,
Of that embalming opiate that allows
Us to navigate beyond our everyday reality
And move into dimensions beyond and asunder!

Use the poppy inside your sacred heart
To say hello to your divine glory;
To express the gratitude for all there is;
For dreams, and otherworldly slumber, make you smart.

Daffodil—*Golden, Honeyed Host*

It must seem like Spring is in the air when you see a "host" of daffodils. The word "host", as used by Wordsworth, is an important one, for it signifies the notion that the daffodils are inviting you, through their golden color, through their honeyed smell, to a party, a party that is being hosted in another dimension by your God self[21].

As you smell the heavenly smell of the daffodil and revel in its golden glory, you find yourself transported to another place in the space/time continuum.

From here you find a matrix where all is seen, all is simultaneous, all is in the NOW. You access, through your multidimensional self, an expansive view of all that provides detachment. The daffodil, the host, transforms into the multiverse that you are very much a part of. For the golden daffodil, the smell of the Creator is within you as well.

And when you find yourself hosted by the daffodil in this new state, in this new dimension, you find that you are one with the host, that you are the host, that all is one, in unity.

Consider your beauty now, your golden glory as a daffodil and let your brightness reach far and wide across the cosmos, attracting others to you in your divinity.

Now, as you return to the Earth, you find yourself transformed by a golden, honeyed glow. You find yourself naturally attracting the bees and those in search of the riches that you have to offer.

And you let them partake, for in doing so you allow them also to start attending the party that you are now hosting. And so, on it goes.

Awaken to your golden rebirthing.

Heliotrope—*Unmasking, Transforming the Demon Within*

My dear Goliath, asking for mercy;
For it is David, indeed, speedy and racy
Who has uncovered your weakness,
Who has unmasked your stress.

For it was stress that made you strive
To be strong, to live out your life
Bullying others into submission,
Overriding their individual mission.

The mercy that David delivers to you
Lies not in whether you live to rue,
Or die to claim your soul anew.
It lies, indeed, in his solar pew;

From which he sends rays of light
To you, to rend you the sight
Of that which is truth,
To release that which is uncouth.

And within this moment of mercy,
Within this moment so cozy,
So intimate within the dance,
Of mortality and your innate stance,

Lies the seed of your transformation,
Lies the seed of your radiation,
Into a new-born emissary of hope;
Into a sun-lighted heliotrope.

So be born anew in fragrant delight;
Enjoy the beauty of radiant sight.
Never fear mortality or pain;
Love can only make you gain.

Forsythia—*Golden Bells Are Ringing*

It must be difficult to understand the ways of the world when you feel trodden down. It must be difficult to reconcile yourself to a fate that seems miserable, unconditionally awful, unconditionally bleak.

It is when you are mired down in this miasma of your own making, this miasma of how awful things are for you, how awful your life is, how awful the future looks, that you are sowing the seeds of your own future destruction, allowing the potentials for growth and expansion to be sucked into the vacuum, the black hole of darkness that surrounds you.

This is the time, dear ones, to reconcile yourself to your existence, to your nature, to your experience, and to the Earth, to Nature. For Nature possesses many healing and alchemical properties. It can transform the dross, the black hole into a crowning emblem of glowing light, and this is what is important for you to seek out when you wallowing in your miasma of disappointment.

See in front of you a bush of flaming, golden yellow forsythia flowers, growing in groups and clumps of sunshiny brightness, spreading an energy of all that is wholesome, all that is glowing, all that is optimistic and excited.

Breathe in the delicious scent of excitement for experience, the excitement for experiencing some of the challenges, some of the dark alleyways you have explored in your life. For these alleyways allow you to see the blockages, the dead-ends, and actually encourage you to seek out the golden, yellow-brick road of your higher destiny, of the higher blueprint your soul would like you to tread, to explore.

The forsythia bush, strikes each of its golden bells in unison, releasing a resonance of sound that vibrates within the very core of your body, awakening in you the inner knowledge of your higher potential, the inner knowledge of your innate mastery, the higher knowledge of your natural state of optimism and excitement.

And as you vibrate in resonance you find the dark, miasmic cloud of disease and disappointment lifting and evaporating from your space. And, as it recedes to the ethers, it is replaced by your own glowing, golden, honeyed, Christ light of unconditional love, acceptance, repentance and resurrection.

For you are renewing and re-enabling that which has been allowed to wither away for many lifetimes, in the dark alleyways and pathways explored in the many lifetimes of dark density on this Earth plane.

But, as the Earth ascends to higher frequencies of light, now, you are opening your own golden bells within your cells, within your DNA, encoded to come forth now, at this time of ascension.

So you now resonate at higher frequencies. And you are attuned and nourished by the golden light and love of Nature. And as you are nurtured by Nature, you discover the lactose, the milk of kindness that is the hallmark of an ascending being, within the Forsythia, within the golden bells.

And, so, now you will transform your miasma into compassion and kindness, first for yourself and then for others. Have compassion for all you have experienced. Be thankful for all you have experienced. And be joyful of the ascending path you are now following.

And so share your nurturing milk of group understanding of the unity of all things and souls and humans through your own forsythia, through your own golden bells. And help the others resonate with you as you all begin to vibrate together in unison, approaching unity.

Forget-Me-Not—*Tantric Communion*

If I were to tell you to let it be,
If I were to tell you to unfold, behold,
All that is in your path, approximately,
You will not stray, you will be sold

To a destiny that is beckoning you;
To a new expression of love
That is challenging many parts of you
To become authentic, to take off the glove.

In the symbol of the blue forget-me-not,
In the confidence of sexual expression,
It conveys through an essence smoking hot,
That burns into your hidden passion,

A tantric identity of wholesome union
With the other; that beautiful part of you
That exists within communion
With another soul, creating unity anew.

And in this new union that is ancient,
And in this old reunion without asperity,
You realize you never forgot, merely sanctioned,
A new blooming, a new expression of totality.

Hyacinth—*Lucky Pattern of Individual Unity*

Just as you want to understand everything in life and sometimes you feel like you understand nothing in life, a hyacinth will first attract you because of its beauty and conical shape and then it will mystify you, because its individual flowers seem to break apart in the pattern. They seem to be assymetrical, although they are very symmetrical within the whole.

So when you admire a hyacinth, or a group of hyacinths, dear ones, we ask that you remember that it is the askew, the off-balance events in life that help create the whole experience that you came here to experience as a soul in this third dimensional density.

Just when you think life is going well, suddenly things might seem to fall apart. A job might disappear, a lover might jilt you, family might disown you or put you down.

And instead of going all askew and letting your life fall apart, we urge you to keep it together. Pull yourself back in, not to your ancestral family, but to the spiritual family that is looking after you all the time. Call on the help and guidance of those whose job it is to assist you in the higher realms. They will provide you with the invisible golden rope to support you, trussing your individual event back up into the whole cone of your life, so that all the slightly askew hyacinths that comprise your many life events become a seamless pattern of conical beauty, reaching up to the heavens, reaching up to the stars.

Anokha. Unique. Yet Part of the One, yet part of all.

That is your journey. That is the journey of all.

Hydrangea—*From Scrooge to a Blooming Community*

As it is sometimes said, "To eat a penny is to eat a dollar." What do we mean by that? When you try to consume your wealth by saving it, by saying: "I want to hoard everything that I have because I don't know what the future will bring, if I will have enough money later", you are saving your pennies, but you are saving your dollars, you are, in a sense, saving too much, and not living in the present, but living in the future.

A hydrangea flower bush is beautiful because it flowers in huge clumps, in all directions, spreading love and beauty and truth about the Creator's vision of all coming together as one, in a mighty burst of color and expressiveness.

So when you try to eat your penny and your dollar, you act in a way that is exactly contrary to the spirit of the Hydrangea, to the spirit of being beautiful, creative, expressive and unified.

You, in a sense, like the miser Scrooge, become an outcast, your particular hydrangea flower loses it color, begins to dry out, falls off the bush and lies hidden in a dark ditch, hoping that in securing a separate place you will survive, in case something happens to the larger plant.

But, as you might suspect, in looking at this isolated flower in a dark ditch, separate from the society of the bush it was once part of and communed with, you are now alone and miserable. You worry even more about your survival, about your pennies, your dollars. In eating your money, you deprive yourself of the water, sunshine and sustenance that is an essential component of being connected to all and to the spiritual part of you.

This is facilitated by community. Community teaches you how to express your spiritual self. How to be compassionate, how to be loving, how to be generous. For, in distancing and isolating yourself, you lose those aspects of yourself that express to others. In becoming the Scrooge of money, you become the Scrooge of spirituality.

Dear one, we beseech you not to dry up with fear and eat your money. Stay connected to the community and to others. Bloom and reflect your beauty as part of the bush. And you will reflect the beauty of the whole, of the cosmos, of the disparity and oneness of all, of the expressive hydrangea bush.

And others will admire you, and you will grow, and, as you grow, the others will grow with you. Nourish one, nourish all. Share and be generous, and your prosperity will grow. Embrace your community, embrace yourself. Collect yourself from your miserly ditch and find solutions with all.

And so you will bloom and transcend the changes that are going on as society transforms.

Poppy Part 2—*Alchemical Transformation of the Self Through Love*

In a pinch, so to speak, we all look for succor and redress. We all look for a way to find the exit, to find the solution, to find the dissolution of the fears that are arising within us.

And, as we examine these fears to try and let them dissipate, we begin to feel even more fearful, and the fears grow larger and bigger, and even more nightmarish doomsday scenarios appear in front of us. I will be evicted from my home. My children will never get the education and the opportunities they deserve. My husband doesn't love me, and our marriage is on the rocks. Take your pick of issue. There is so much that humans worry about and want to dissipate. That is when they seek an opiate.

And the opiate does not need to be the opium from the poppy flower exclusively. There are many opiates available today to the modern man and woman. Tranquillizers and painkillers abound. Antidepressants abound. Even erectile dysfunction chemical tablets are a form of opiate, substituting chemical alchemy for natural tantric alchemy.

And, in each case of the easy kill, the easy destruction of the fear with those pills, comes the side effect of the self-destruction of your DNA, of your cells, of your mitochondria. And this can be a telling fate. And this can delay your awakening. And this can delay your ascension.

So, as you seek your opiate, and put yourself to sleep, you are hearkening your own death, for your life becomes a purgatory, one that is not worth living, one that is not real. But one you keep replaying again and again, without any succor, without any redress.

So let us instead encourage you to smell the poppy flower and admire its beauty; not for its opiate, but for its intrinsic self. It is beautiful and comes in many colors and varieties. And it is a flower of love. And it is a flower of death. And it is a flower of resurrection.

So find yourself now transported to the poppy field within Oz. And you might find within yourself a sense of trepidation, of fear, that yes, indeed, death has come to claim me. Yes, indeed, that is fate and dissolution knocking on my door. And as you lie down to sleep amongst these beautiful flowers, you indeed fall asleep.

But you are awakened shortly by sunlight streaming into your eyes and covering your body in a golden, shimmering, shower of light and delight. For you are being resurrected, you are being reborn through the power of love. Soak it in, dear ones, and believe that you are starting a new incarnation, a new life, within the same body that you had before. All will change, all is changing, as the Shift proceeds.

And, as you now begin to recognize that you are much grander and more powerful than you think, that you have many more talents and skills than you think, you realize that the poppy's secret is the transformative power of the vibration of love that it carries.

Just as we often wear poppies on our lapels as a symbol of support and honoring for those who are hewed down by life, whether by disease or war, we now wear our love for ourselves on our lapels, and use the love of the poppy flower to unfold our very own special beauty and smell.

And we find that we no longer need an opiate. We no longer need to calm our fears. For we are on a natural high. We are our own aphrodisiac. And we join a human tantric ecstasy of being that is happy, enlightened and benign.

Welcome to a higher dimensional frequency.

Throat Chakra
Beech Tree—Logos of Life in Your Throat Chakra

If you try to understand why life takes you in a certain direction with a logical mind, you will tie yourself up in knots. You will try and analyze and dissect events in a linear way. You will try and make sense of a journey that is actually spiral-like in form, leading you through turns and cycles to new pathways of growth and evolution. For, as you take new turns, you gain new perspectives, new insights.

And instead of analyzing, cogitating, worrying about meaning, we would encourage you instead to simply express your experience and share it with others. It is in describing what you have gone through, what you are going through, and what you will be going through, that you connect with the rest of humanity, your brethren, and you give them insights by courageously sharing your specific challenges, your specific successes.

And so we would compare this innate instinct within you to share, to discuss with others, to the beautiful, shady, restful beech tree. This is a tree that has provided the shade and repose for many to simply sit still, to let the analytical, cogitating dross drop away, to let the left brain go to sleep, alighting within the right brain, the creativity that then can come forth through myriad forms of expression: singing, poetry, art, music, drama, novels, stories, kabuki theatre.

For what the beech tree does is it stimulates those aspects of your throat chakra that connect to the Universal mind of all there is.

You connect to the archetypes that Plato said existed before time and space, and, indeed, he was right[22]. You connect to a flowing, pan-cosmic river of knowledge that you can fill a cup from to bring in information about your human experience, knowing that the river will always flow with enough water for all, that the cup never runneth dry, for the bounty of infinity can never be circumscribed.

And you give these eternal forms a manifestation that belies your very experience, your very turn around the spiral, your completely unique expression.

So cogitate now on the beauty of your connection to Source through the lines of energy that come into your throat chakra. Spread the shade, the beauty of the beech tree by sharing your vision, your thoughts and your experiences; not by analyzing, not by using facts and figures, but by expressing innate understanding.

And, indeed, use metaphors and glyphs and symbols and logos. For all language stems originally from sound, vibration, and analogy. The expression of universal, higher-dimensional consciousness first took shape in pictorial forms such as Sanskrit.

And it is said that the first words of Sanskrit were inscribed on a beech tree. And perhaps you might note that the word "book", in old English, traces its origin from the same etymological source as beech.

And, so, be not austere in your communication in the world. Be not parsimonious in sharing your human, your worldly experience. Simply call on your connection to the river of plenty, to the river of creativity, cloak it with your vibrations, decorate your unique vessel you hold it in, and offer this new holy grail to all, to share.

For each sip, in each of its myriad forms from different human experiences, adds to the Universal knowledge and understanding of Source experiencing itself.

For you are a part of God, and as you express your logos, you create new worlds and new understandings.

And, so, a new genesis begins.

Chapter 6
Growing Out of the Nest

Parakeet—*Familiarity Absconds Reality*

Ordinarily one would want to buy a parrot as a pet, not a parakeet. A child has heard of a parrot, it knows that the parrot can make strange, mimicking sounds. It knows that a parrot can be fun.

But it does not know what a parakeet is. It does not know that this is another form of a parrot, that this bird, too, can make special sounds. And that this bird is unique, different from a parrot in its plumage, in its history and its growth.

And so the child, might simply dismiss a parakeet as a pet, choosing the parrot instead, for it seems more familiar, more instantly accessible.

And so, dear ones, like a child, you often choose the next step in life as being that which is most familiar, that which is most known, and in so doing you find yourself excluding the exotic, even though the exotic itself is important.

And when you exclude the exotic, you are, in a sense, excluding what could become your familiar in the future, as your spiritual self grows, and your vibrational needs are enhanced.

For a parakeet can act as a familiar, as a parrot-plus antenna that will connect you to your guides at a slightly more refined level, that will bring in information for you, through its odd statements, through its moods that are more appropriate for you, as you go through more refined and more well-tuned parts of your spiritual journey.

So, dear ones, as you choose your next adventure or mission or project in life, dare to extend yourself beyond your immediate familiar, beyond that which breeds familiarity, to a sense of a new kind of familiar that acts as an antenna, attracting new vibrations in a familiar way to accentuate your growth.

Choose the trip to the Sahara instead of to Ohio. Go bunjee jumping instead of taking a subway ride. Scream your lungs out at a karaoke bar instead of staying hushed inside a museum.

And what was familiar before recedes as what was exotic before becomes familiar to the new you who has grown through the experience of the parakeet, of the exotic, of that which seemed different, but was actually perfect for you.

And so you skip along, the child in you growing, not to adulthood and conformity, but to a playful, more fully-developed child that actually releases the cultural programming that says: "you must do what is familiar, what is accepted".

You return to the more spiritual child that was originally born, wanting to taste, touch and smell all there is in this wonderful adventure called life on planet Earth.

And that seems familiar.

Sparrow—*Divine Providence Delivered*

In a sense, the sparrow is the downtrodden hero of old, the poor peasant, the unbeknowst being that will be cared for by God, by the Creator, as Christ has noted in the Bible[23].

This sparrow has a lore of being unassailable, of being unrepentant in its desire for the noblesse oblige to oblige it with succor and with success. This sparrow has a history of not giving up, of being the bird of a non-partisan singularity of mind to get what is believes it is owed.

And, in the cities of the world, sparrows have now become ubiquitous, determined foragers amongst the spoils of the messy humans all around, surviving in a world that does not seem to care.

And so we say to you, as you feel sometimes that you are scavenging around in your life, trying to find a lifeline, trying to search for help, trying to find the gift-bearer for your survival, you may sometimes identify with the ubiquitous sparrow that is ignored, is plentiful and often taken for granted.

Hamlet once said that "there is a divine providence" in sparrows[24], and we say to you that there is a divine providence in you.

Just as a sparrow will always be able to forage and survive, you too are tough as nails and can get through any challenges that come your way.

Know that the providence Hamlet refers to is not just a nameless God or Creator who cares for you. This is a providence that accepts that you designed the outlines of your life plan, of your life plot, before you were born. That you chose to insert several challenges in your life, where you would feel like a ubiquitous sparrow, unnoticed, unclaimed, unbethrothed. And that part of your life's journey is to embrace these challenges as lessons.

For the providence of the Creator is such that you would never have been allowed to create a plan or draw to you a challenge that you could not live up to, that you could not face.

So disavow your sense of victimhood, of being second-class, of being the peasant that has to be observed and saved by the Creator. Know that your tenacity, your ability to power through your challenges will allow you always find a solution and move forward.

For, dear ones, you are the very providence you seek, you are the very Creator you try to seek succor and redress from above. You are the creator of your destiny, and, like the sparrow, you will always prevail.

Your divine providence is such that your learning will help your soul grow, moving you to higher and higher vibrations, moving you to ethereal expressions of your divine being. And so it is. And so it must be.

And this is the divine providence of the sparrow as prophesized by Christ and anointed by Hamlet.

Starling—*Resist Not A Call to Your Star Family*

In a pinch one can always ask for help. When one feels like there are no options available, that doom is part of one's imminent destiny, that is the time to pick up the phone and ask for help.

That is the time to reach out to a relative, to a neighbor and say "This is my predicament. This is my sorrow. Help me, please, if you can."

And you might be surprised at how helpful humanity is at heart. Although you might need to swallow your pride to ask for help, those who you ask might well provide a helping hand, a lending hand, a hand of support.

They are like the starling family that you belong to. Like stars from the far corners of the Universe, you have all come here to play a game, to take a part in the theatre of your life, as played out on the Earth plane. And as stars, deep down inside, you are pure love and you get great satisfaction from helping others and from being of service.

And, a starling, the bird incarnation of that star, is also a social, helpful bird. It sings its song and it socializes with other starlings. Together, in flocks, they feed and they collect and forage food for their young. These star-flecked birds have a lesson for you, dear one. You cannot do it all alone. Call on your star family for help. Call on the human spirit to be of plentiful, heartfelt amity for you.

For in the amity that you ask for and you will eventually receive, you create a bond, an etheric union between yourself and this other member of your starling family that allows you to vibrate in a higher frequency as you both express the connection that exists between all souls in higher dimensions. This bond is appealing and will attract others who want to be part of this bond, this growing network of light and love.

And so your starling family grows, and so your starlight increases, and so the plumage of your aura glows with starry lights and guides who wish to be around your ever-growing conscious ability to transcend the illusions of the daily life and see everything from a more familial perspective.

Smile bright and hold hands with the other stars in your human family. For you are all stars, you are all heroes for valiantly choosing to incarnate on Earth and help with the Ascension of the planet at this time.

And know that you are all in this together. Act like a family and work well together. Love each other. And help each other.

And soon you will find the compassionate Buddha within you is an everyday occurrence, as natural as the starlight that enters your perception over the horizon every single night.

Glow bright and sing a song of family. For your sense of self, your sense of group consciousness is awakening.

Magpie—*Reveling, Revealing a Maverick Within*

Ordinarily, a magpie is resistant to change. It wants to have everything its own way. It likes to scavenge its own way. It likes to build nests in its own way. It likes to forage in its own way. It is, so to speak, a maverick, a leader, a creator of that which is perfect for itself.

And it is a fantastic role model for us as we move forward with the many changes that we see going on around us in our lives. For, like a magpie, we, too, must be confident in our individuality, in our own unique way of approaching any task in life, whether it involves food, sex, creativity or simply friendship.

It is in the very individual flavor of our expression that we can gain confidence and a sense of verisimilitude[25] in the face of adversity.

For adversity and challenge is a given and a constant in life, dear ones. Know that adversity and challenges are part of the game of life that you signed up for before you incarnated. Yes, of course there will be happy and successful times in your life. But there will also be times when others tell you that you need to change, that the way you are doing things is not right, will lead to your ruin.

And this is where the verisimilitude of the magpie will serve you very well. As a totem, the magpie teaches you that your versatility in handling life is unbounded. There are skills and talents hidden within you that will help you to explore and conquer every single example of adversity and challenge that comes your way. And you will do this with panache, with your own style, your own unique expression.

The biggest challenge that might befall you and might, in a sense, arrest you, is your own lack of confidence or lack of belief in yourself.

If you do not believe, as the magpie does, that your knowledge about how to take care of yourself is better than any other person's opinions, you might relinquish that inner knowledge, that inner being back to a locked box and never turn the key. You might choose to follow another's guidelines, which might never really fit you, which might, in a sense, confine you, limit you.

So if ever you feel that life is not letting you grow, not letting you expand, not letting you be blissful, the first step to take is to take a look at yourself in the mirror.

And just as a magpie, the intelligent bird that it is, is able to recognize itself and its own leadership, look lovingly into your own eyes and say out aloud: "I am the creator of my reality. I am the leader of my life. I am the revealer of my destiny. I ask the Creator to find ways to unveil to my many gifts and talents so that I can express my true creator self, and be of service to the world. That is what I came here for. And I will take the risk. I will become the maverick who believes in his or her own ability and way of tackling a task. And so be it."

And so it shall be, dear ones. Learn about self-confidence from the magpie. And forage and build your life through experience in a self-confident and inimitable manner. And much will come your way in a flow that is magical and mirroring your true destiny.

Swan—*Golden Rebirthing*[26]

Once upon at time of old
There was a maiden made of gold.
Golden was her beauty,
Swan-like was her neck;
And within the confines of her body,
Much beauty and fire made her bold.

Her name was Leda, a maiden pure;
Ever so sweet, ever so demure.
She lay upon the banks of a river,
Expecting to see the swans a-stir.
A swan indeed did bestir withal:
It was Zeus who came to be her cure.

Disguised as a swan, he her besmote,
Drowning her in the muddy moat
Of life and duality; for through her
Ravishment came war and grief and misery.
And through her offspring
Much suffering and disaster the world did note.

But, now, as we have travelled through
The eons of duality and warfare,
Now that we have traversed the game
Of hate, desire, futility and fright,
Now comes the time to hope anew
We have left behind the times to rue.

For a new ravishment of golden sight
Is approaching our darkly blight.
No instance of prior inhabitation

Could prepare for this divine visitation
Of celestial insight and creation,
To discover our inner swan and might.

O Masters of old, O Spirits from afar
You are eternal, you are grand.
You are here to change this game
From the duality that Zeus wrought
To a new age of grace and agility;
To a time of love and community.

Peacock—*Uncloak your 100 Eyes*[27]

Furthermore is a word that conveys the sense of distance and of plenty. Furthermore, they say, such and such will happen. Furthermore, in days of old, the ancient men would convey their sense of wisdom, their sense of discipline, their sense of duty that was to be required of all initiates.

For, indeed, duties and unfettered obedience were the characteristics of those days. And there were those who were cloistered and those who donned the robes to devote themselves to lives of servitude and service, and, in so doing, cut themselves off from the larger aspect of life, the aspect of life that touches all of humanity, and hence is all-knowing, all-awakened.

And, indeed, it is now time to shun and discard the old robes and cloaks of yore which yoked you to a particular master, to a particular teaching whose vocabulary included the vibration of "furthermore".

And if it is distance and plenty that you seek, might we redirect you to the distance of the heavens, of the higher dimensions, and the abundance of the Universe, which is limitless and provides plenty for all.

And as you now discard the old and look towards the new, you find that you do not need any new clothes, you do not need any coverings. For what lies beneath, in your true nakedness of your true, divine self is a sleeping beauty of wonderful delight and insight.

For, like a peacock of ancient times, you are already wise, you are already masterful, you can already see afar, and you already are wealthy. For it is through the 100 eyes that you radiate to the world, in your feathers abloom, that you muster the courage to alight in the world and anchor in the world the energies of the Creator anew.

No longer is it the time to be cloistered in your temples and your churches and your constricted trappings of ancient religions and teachings. No longer is it the time to be put into the straitjacket of confinement and infinite piety that associates deprivation with ascension, and duty and obedience with growth.

Alight anew into your existing plumage. Follow the lines of wisdom and insight that blaze forth from each of your 100 eyes of vision. And you will see clearly and you will see afar. You will discover ancient wisdom that was always there and always will be. And this ancient wisdom will be malleable, adaptable for the modern world.

You might seek the ancient mysteries of Egypt and of Horus. You might seek the ancient Vedic scriptures of the creation of existence. You might seek the truth of life within the resurrection of the Christ.

But each of these ancient teachings can be updated, with the wisdom that is inside. Each of these teachings can be loosened, so that the outer shrouding can be released, so that the robes can be flung afar, and the connection inside you which knows more than any ancient teaching might have conveyed in written form, is nakedly shown, is nakedly shared and so enflames and engulfs humanity with new levels of conscious awareness and new levels of spiritual and religious understanding.

For one is simply a higher aspect of the other. For one simply, with your 100 peacock eyes, allows you to see further and bring in more.

Bathe in the glory of yourself and enjoy your naked beauty. It is time to celebrate; it is time to spread the wealth.

Chapter 7
The Fruits of Amelioration

Lemon—*Nostalgia Creates Anew*

Nostalgia is an important element in life. When one is passing through a new phase, a turbulent time of change, it is common to think back about the good old times, when you were a child, when you were on vacation, when you first kissed a loved one with passion.

And it is when those moments of nostalgia help you to remember the past in a positive way that you are, in a sense, allowing the emotions from that past to infiltrate your present. And in so doing you can recreate, redefine your present experience.

It is almost like the passion, the happiness, the golden moment of the past is like a piece of lemon which is squeezed on to a serving that life has put on your plate today. It adds that touch of acidity that make the present moment tastier, better placed in context, better set for the future in that the platform is now attainable, flexible and springy.

And you might find yourself asking for a cup of tea to sooth you through the turbulence of change; and it is when you add the lemon of happy nostalgia to your tea of the moment, that you find the health benefits of remembering and transforming the past.

What is important is to find that moment of passion, that squirt of lemon from the past and remember the emotions, the feelings. Bring those feelings back into your present moment and imagine them spreading out in lines of lemony energy out towards your future, creating the emotional basis for your future creations, your future destiny, your future adventures.

But we caution you, dear one, to not get stuck in the past. Do not stay in that happy memory so long that you do not want to come back. And that is why we suggest the lemony aspect of this alchemy. For when you take too much lemon, add too many squirts to anything, it overwhelms that taste of what you were originally trying to enhance. Acidity becomes truly acidic. So we suggest that nostalgia, memory, is powerful, when used judiciously.

And what power it is! For, dear one, you have the power to completely choose your future, creating it based on your emotions, and using the past to feel the emotions that are best suited for your journey.

We hope and pray that you will embrace this wonderful new role you have as co-creators in your destiny in this wonderful new world that we are all moving to.

Lick your lips and taste the lemon of cleanliness, of health, of memory and passion. And create your next step among your many options as you continue down the pathways of your life.

Blackberry—*Re-vision Your Communication*

In the event that one feels nostalgic for the past, for a moment that has gone by, for a sense of passion, for an emotion, for a friendship, you now know that there are ways to find that feeling once again from the past, and manifest it not only in your present, but also in your future.

Just as a blackberry, as used in the office, and now in daily life, is a means for communication with everyone, helping you keep track of your emails and correspondence, knowing what is next to do on your to-do list, so you can eat a blackberry fruit piece or pieces to connect with elements of your past, and communicate with it, bringing it into your present, and projecting it into your future.

As you bite into the luscious black and blueness of the blackberry you, in a sense, blot out the veils that create the illusion of time. In blotting out the veils, you encounter a matrix of many colors, but no black, and, within this matrix, in this absence of black, blotted out by the incipient and insouciant taste of the blackberry, you find the potential, the emotion that existed in the past and you can access it and feel it from your current moment.

For it in the thesis and its antithesis that we often find a synthesis.

The blackberry is dark, unknowable, yet tangy, delicious. Its darkness allows us to pierce the illusions that were not seen before, and, in so doing, we access the colors in a new synthesis. The colors of all there is. The colors of the Creator. The colors of a reality that is always in the NOW, always accessible.

So bite into that blackberry and connect with your past, and free yourself from the illusion. And the natural blackberry is much more suited for this task than the blackberry that you use while you are in your suit in the office. For that blackberry perpetuates the illusion that everything is within a time loop, that everything must be scheduled, that everything has its place and order in a linear fashion. The dark blotter of the blackberry fruit shatters these illusions and transports you to a higher knowing.

Now you recognize the emotions and sentiments of love and sharing and caring. And you choose to release the pain and limitation of the past.

And in choosing the thesis of that which is life-affirming, rejecting the antithesis, which is life-draining, and in creating the new colored matrix synthesis beyond the veils of time, you can create and manifest a perfect future for yourself, claiming only that which is perfect your destiny, and for your inexorable growth as a soul in search of a transmission and connection and communication in an expansive way with all that is.

Raspberry—*Indicate Who You Are, Facilitate Your Survival*

Just as one wants to often break down and cry and break apart into a 100 pieces of self-inflicted pain, the raspberry, in its network of carefully patterned drupelets, each surrounding a central core, and woven into a symmetrical, oval-shaped pattern, is fragile, and can easily be crushed, each of its 100 drupelets dissolved, broken apart, mutilated[28].

But what holds this raspberry together? What makes its fragility and squishiness part of its very being, yet allows it to survive and be a source of nourishment for others?

It is both the exquisite patterns it exhibits and, then, the care that the pickers impart on it because they know of its worth, know that there is a large demand out there for this vital source of antioxidants, anti-inflammation and anti-cancer fighting agents.

As knowledge about the raspberry's many beneficial qualities has grown, this has only enhanced the older understanding of its beauty, of its fragility, of its taste.

And so, dear ones, for those of you who rely on external validation, based on your appearance, we would like you to consider that just as the raspberry is fragile and held together by the symmetry of the creator, you, too, are fragile and held together by the symmetry of the creator, and you also do not need external validation to survive.

What you need to rely on instead is that inner beauty, that inner source of protein and health-inducing agents that nourish both yourself and others.

A lot of your talents, your strengths, your abilities have never been acknowledged by you. And if they have never been acknowledged by you, how can they be acknowledged by someone else?

For, dear one, instead of thinking about the 100 pieces you might break apart into, cogitate instead upon the 100 unique gifts and talents you bring to the earth, each with its own harmony and set of health-inducing and producing skills, each part of the entire being of that which is you, made greater as a whole, made more beauteous in one woven pattern; made more efficacious and more efficient as one being.

So step forth with confidence, not self-derisively. Step forward with abundance, not poverty. Step forward with alacrity, not soberness. And partake of the world, sharing your inner, hidden gifts and treasures. For you came here to do so. You came here to show yourself, even though you are and feel fragile, even though you are and can be crushed, mutilated.

But it is your intention to be and not dissolve, to co-exist with a sometimes harsh world that will sustain you and your ever-glorious beauty in a world that is full of surprise and the unexpected.

And just as the raspberry, in its infinite beauty and fragility makes its way to the consumer's palate nourishing him or her with many hidden health benefits, even though it might have been crushed so many times along the way on it journey by so many clumsy hands, you, too, will make your way through a path that has many challenges. But, with your intention, you will not break apart, you will not fall down and cry.

For your beauteous raspberry red of filial duty and prestigious righteousness will be righted into a more intact raspberry red of self-duty and non-committal heralding of that which is obvious: your hidden and obscured, but now loudly proclaimed gifts and talents.

Stay intact, stay proud, stay abreast of the world and herald the redness of your 100 talents, of the 100 drupelets of your raspberry glory.

Tomato—*Bursting Forth into Group Consciousness*

Read in the name of thy Lord. This is an injunction that has been given before, for the monotheistic case, for the cultural origins of literacy, for the assimilation of spirituality into the ground, this Earth plane, Gaia.

And indeed, that is what people have done over time, to expand their consciousness. They have read the scriptures, they have read the supposed words of God, some of which were true, and some of which were downloaded and recorded by inauthentic forces, that were trying to pervert the true words of Spirit, that were trying to ensure that this game of dark and light would spiral further down into the darkness, and not spiral up, into the light.

For, like the tomato's lusciousness and its beauty and its healthy qualities are delivered upon eating, it must first grow through the ground, the underground, the dark, and that is where it must be nourished in order to sprout.

Each individual human consciousness is like a luscious, ripe tomato that is about to be born, that is about to break ground and come forth into the sunlight. Part of the game, however, has been to spend time in the muck, amongst the worms, amongst the manure, amongst the darkness.

And, although that journey in itself has had its very unpleasant moments, and, although darkness has clouded and ruined your parade many a time, know that it is though this journey of darkness that you have prepared yourself for this moment of ascension, to come forth now and offer your luscious tomato fruit to the heavens.

In a sense, the timing is such that it aligns with major changes on the Galactic, cosmic clock. There are many alignments going on, dear ones. Alignments around the galactic center, alignments around your universal center. It is as if many revolutions of long durations are now synchronizing in a moment that comes around once in an eon.

And this eon, as has always been planned, is the time to stop this particular game, for it has indeed gone too far.

It is now time, indeed, to harvest the fruit, of many years of labour and tilling the fields with manure and raindrops of tears and pain and suffering. For every dear human soul has a red, luscious heart bursting with the love of the red rose deep inside. Each human soul's true nature is that of beauty, is that of voluptuousness, sensuality, sun-ripening, and juiciness. And like a tomato, each human readily offers it nutritious and delicious taste to all those who wish to taste it.

And this is not a sacrifice, dear ones, for in becoming part of who it has been offered to, the human soul grows in its merging, for merging allows the harvesting and incipient formation of a group consciousness. And becoming a group consciousness is part of the ascension. And as this happens repeatedly, the consciousness will begin to notice that it is part of a larger vine of many tomatoes, all connected in an ever-ascending spiral.

You are about to spiral up dear ones. You are about to go home. It is ascension time.

Pear—*Milky, Nurturing Fruit of the Creator*

On a mountaintop one feels one can see forever. Vistas of beauty of all that there is flash in bursts of brightness into our vision, into our memory, into our fantasies of the future. It is a moment to be cherished.

Yet, the journey up to the top of this mountain sometimes seems endless, sometimes feels fatiguing, sometimes feels pointless. It is a neverending target, forever disappearing as we appear to ascend, although we sometimes feel that we actually drop down into a never before anticipated valley.

And it is when you are in this valley that it is useful to take a bite of the milky, silky pear. This fruit of the Creator is a portal that through its taste suggests a nurturing, a coddling that is maternal and comforting to you as you taste a softness, a silkiness, a fairy dust spreading all over you, as you twinkle in delight.

Know that the Creator has embedded in the pear, the nurturing essence of the Milky Way, of the galaxy that you now inhabit. As you taste the pear, its softness is disarming; its taste is appealing, yet mild. In a way it is the perfect laxative to help you unleash and release those fears and worries that have allowed you to descend into your valley of twilight.

And it is within the crepuscular twilight that the pear shines a light of nurturing growth, providing a beam, a path for a new place for you to look, for you to place your attention. You feel nurtured, and you look up to thank the Mother of all that is for this fruit, for this gift.

And in looking up, you see the vestige of your next destination, of your next stop of this path up the mountain of your journey to your ascension to a higher dimension. You find the pear path light shining the way in a soothing, nurturing way.

So take the next step, find the nurturing qualities within yourself that the pear has engendered. Nurture your inner child, allow it to release any fears and disease and lack of belief that have come up. And beam yourself up in the nurturing light of the Creator to your next step. And breathe and taste the milk of purity, the milk of no acerbity, the milk of alacrity.

And you are on your way now back on your journey up the mountaintop.

Pineapple—*Honey and Manna from Reconstitution*

Just as when a bee bites a human and then there is that initial rush of pain followed by remorse, or the emotion of why did this happen to me, so, when a person who is not attuned to the taste of a pineapple, or even allergic to it, is accidentally allowed to bite into a morsel of this delicious, unique tropical fruit, that person also feels an initial rush of pain, a sense of this is not right for me, I should have avoided this incident.

But, dear ones, it is not about avoiding unpleasant incidents in life that makes life safe or meaningful. It is quite the opposite. It is when unpleasant, accidental events take place that there appears an opportunity to explore why there was a negative reaction, and embrace the experience and grow exponentially.

Let us explain. Whenever a human has a strong reaction to an event, or an unpleasant reaction, there is a reason that is far greater than just that particular incident. There might have been a past life where emotion around that event or piece of fruit, for example, might have locked in a distaste, a reaction, an allergy.

The human who accidentally bit into the pineapple might have been force-fed pineapple as a prisoner, once a week, in a past lifetime. Trust us, dear ones, there is a person who had this experience, while incarnating in the Amazon. So this person is given a small amount of fruit to survive on, and nothing else, except a few sips of water here and there. And so this person begins to crave this fruit, yet also loathes it, for it represents his captivity, his enslavement.

And so, in a current incarnation, his body will remember the abuse that it was subjected to when it ate the pineapple, and so it will go into shock, into reaction.

Similarly, when a bee bites a human, the body might remember a time when a more potent bee attack by a swarm occurred and go into an allergic reaction, with rashes all over the body.

But the bee sting can be calmed by balms. The stinger can be removed. And it will heal eventually, allowing the person to focus on that pain, unearthing the reason for it, and hence permanently extracting it from their body's memory, from the spiral of DNA and RNA that accompanies them on every incarnation.

So it is that the person who hates eating pineapple, in biting into it, might use the taste as an opportunity to tune into the past lifetime that might be the source of this distaste. If the person cannot do this alone, past-life regressions, or simply approaching a clairvoyant energy healer might be an option.

Let us assure you that such measures will be much more effective than going to the allergist's office, getting multiple shots, and trying to figure out what your body is allergic to.

For, dear ones, there is much more to your body than its allergies. There is much more to your permanent Higher Self than the trivial traumas that become embedded in it as part of the game that humans play of hurting each other.

So let go of the past. Forgive and forget and heal that which might be hidden in the dark recesses of your psyche.

Embrace the honey of the honeybee, not its sting. Embrace the vibrant vibration of the pineapple, not the fact that it is a foreign taste, or too acidic, or that you might react to it.

Step out of reaction, and into creation, dear ones. For now is the time to create a whole new you. Anything is possible.

Pine Tree—Transgressing and Weaving a New Reality with Your 3rd Eye

In a pinch, we seek to find a solution. When life pinches us, poking its pine needles into our daily skin, we feel the need to break new ground, to explore new pathways of expressing, of being, of connecting.

And so, a pine tree in its spiraling shape and spiraling expression of cones and leaves and needles, too, expresses a need to supersede, to transgress and to evolve beyond the mundane, beyond the everyday pinches that are growing and embedded everywhere within its body. For the pine knows that it is in accepting the needles, the barbs that we can grow higher and spread the shade for others, to overcome any hidden shadows.

So embed this image of the pine tree within your third eye, within the width and breadth of your forehead. For it is in the broad array of your higher consciousness, it is within this broad array of connecting and seeing in metaphysical and quantum ways that you will supersede, that you will transgress, that you will evolve beyond the pine needles that are poking you in your everyday life.

And indeed, sometimes it feels like there is no solution, that you are cornered like an animal being led to the ritual slaughter in a tedious life of no freedom, no creativity, no absolution.

And this is when you transform your pine needles into spindles that spread out and weave lines of masterful energy from the broad array of your crown chakra. Your broadleaf, evergreen leaves are now serving a new function, a metaphysical function, a quantum function.

They are sending our rays from your personal array to the arrays of connection in the 3rd eyes of others, of Gaia, of the Spirit beings of the light who provide guidance, and of the higher cosmic intelligence of all there is.

And in so doing, you draw back towards yourself a line of insight, a line of delight, a line that forms part of the weaving that your spindle is spinning. For it is within this very weaving of the new form of being that your transform yourself, that you evolve yourself, by transgressing the limitations of what can and cannot be, that have been imposed on you.

Like a superhuman you clairvoyantly assess your options, you bring in quantum insights, you supercede your reality.

And may your third eye be forever evergreen. May the broad array of your forehead always celebrate the broad nature of its multifarious connections. May your golden spindle weave golden webs of connections up and down the cosmos and in every direction in between. For as a master weaver of the light, you can completely sublimate any irritation that might have pined into you.

For, instead of pining for a different future, instead of wailing as if you might have been led to the strictures of ritual slaughter, you now weave away and use your pine leaves to direct the energy where it can best serve you.

And you resurrect yourself without dying. For you are simply seeing with the unseen eye what was always there. And, so, you spiral up, and you evolve to higher dimensions of reality and of consciousness.

Chapter 8
Colors for Divining

Vermilion—*Ordinary Twilight Bewitching Summons a Higher Self*

Immense as it might seem, the desire to commune with the Creator, to really understand your source, from whence you came, and to where you are going, is a natural one, and one that can be satisfied with growing ease as you become more spiritual, more open to the natural world and the wonder of your earthly life experience.

There was once a Hindu man who searched his entire life for this sense of communion, of a delicious revelation that would give meaning to the daily grind, the daily tasks that befell him every day. These were ancient times, and there was quite a lot of openness to seeing beyond the veils of illusion that define your reality. So he sat down under a tree and he silenced all around him and within him and through him and eventually he found that communion, that deep, delicious connection with the spiritual world that can provide a perspective that puts your life's experiences within context, and gives them meaning. Let us just say that this man's communion led to a worldwide teaching about breaking free from **samsara** and embracing your incarnation within the wheels of reincarnation.

We say unto you that the color vermilion, that delicious in-between red and orange color of twilight and a crepuscular glory, is an entry point for you to commune, to break through the samsara, to find the bridge to a spiritual reality that will allow you to gloriously claim your everyday experience as a fantastic reality of being that ennobles you and allows you to grow.

Just as the twilight, heralded by the vermilion colors of a sunset, is bewitching and magical, so the color vermilion bewitches you into a portal of access to your inner being, to your guides and to your sense of otherwordly creation that opens your eyes in a new and deeply silent and satisfying way.

And so, as you, like a Hindu, symbolically dip the vermilion color of Sindhoo on your forehead, or in the parting of your hair, you express this twilight, this magical desire and eventual crossing into higher levels of understanding and reality. And soon, the ritual, which can be an etheric one as well, allows you, automatically to access the other dimensions, the voices of your guides and of the Creator more easily, more like a **bodhisattva.**

And, so, you, with your everyday vermilion anointing, in seeking to be that which you already are, find yourself becoming an everyday **Buddha**, a compassionate observer of your own life and of others.

And, hence, you become a teacher; for in your stillness, in your compassion, in your delicious vermilion access to higher reality, you provide the example for others to follow as they try to divine your secret and hence give themselves permission to ask for a portal to your vermilion sanctity.

Lilac—*A Lighter Path to Honeyed, Cinnamoned Acceptance of Sanctity*

Assumptions are often made about the sanctity of life. About how it is so precious that it must never be wasted, whether through euthanasia, or through abortion.

These pro-lifers, in a sense, drain all the life out of life with their rigidity, with their close-mindedness. For life is about choice, choice to conceive, choice to leave, choice to be aborted, to say, no, it is time to go home.

And so, these pro-lifers end up draining the violet sanctity of life. They violate the covenant of souls to live and let live. They drain the sanctity of their love of the Creator to a lilac color, one that is a faded purple, one that has remnants of glory, but seems to be a pale residue of what it should be.

Similarly, dear ones, on a larger, more expansive scale, organized religions have a tendency to remove the lifeblood of spirituality by their insistence on the sacred, on ritual, on giving up your authority to recognized, ordained elders in the religion. They ask of their followers to follow blindly, smudging them with smoke and mirrors, the sacred becoming desecrated, the violet becoming a pale lilac, waiting to be resuscitated.

And, dear ones, we wish to assure you that lilac is indeed a beautiful color of the creator, wistful and lilting, expressive and subtle. What matters is the road you take to this vibration that affects how you experience it.

If you choose to be restricted by religion, by conformity, by dogma and you drain yourself into a giving lilac by giving up your power, you will never flower, never bloom, and you will feel frustrated, you will feel restrained, you will feel a tad under the weather.

But if you choose to find a lightness within yourself, allow yourself to take your spirituality, your love of the Creator and all of his creations into a bubbly, airy format, you find yourself allowing your sense of sanctity for the divine moving to a lighter color, a lilac of air brightness and fulsome love.

Like a rising soufflé, you desire to express yourself beautifully and you rise to the occasion, filtering a lilac smell of honeyed love and cinnamoned acceptance of others.

And as you now have chosen this lighter path to the lilac of your soul, you, in your self-knowledge and light acceptance of others, forgive those who tried to constrain you earlier, who tried to tell you how to think, who tried to control your sexuality, your ability to have or not have children, your ability to say I am moving on from my life.

For you know that they are simply mired in an illusion, a wrap of violet haze that they mistake for sanctity, but is actually a velvet glove of shame. For it is through shame that you give up your power. And it is through a sweet, honeyed, cinnamoned lightness that you reclaim it, in full, sanctimonious, lilac beauty.

Platinum—*Join the Inclusive Angelic Choir*

Ordinarily one doesn't use platinum in one's life every day. It is a precious metal, one which is not easily mined, not easily found, not easily provided. And so, it is a metal of not ubiquity but of selectivity. It is a proud moment when you are invited to join the Platinum round of an event, the Platinum level of a membership, and the Platinum level of a choir.

And the choir that we are referring to, dear ones, is the choir of heavenly voices that lilt and sing praises and prayers to the high heavens. We refer to those angelic beings of light that with their silvery voices, catapult themselves to the highest levels of spiritual mastery and access, the highest levels of spiritual glory, the highest levels of spiritual contact.

And so, as you move along on your path of ascension, as you move upwards and bring Spirit downwards into your body, there will come a time when you will be recognized as a Master, there will come a time when you will join the angelic choir of God's glory; yet, paradoxically, you will still be human, you will still be incarnate.

Welcome to the ascension, dear one. You will have ascended to the Platinum level of spiritual attainment, you would have joined the angelic hierarchy, and you would stay on the earth to be the example to others, to transfer these platinum energies through your physical presence to others, so that they themselves might awaken, that they themselves might take the steps so essential to their own mastery and growth, through the various colors and levels, through, silver and gold and finally platinum levels of spiritual attainment.

And you, in your platinum mastery, become the precious metal, the precious being of light that will conduct spiritual light to all, that will not get corroded, that will not get oxidized. You, in your platinum voice, will provide a new set of overtones to the existing angelic choir, providing a resonance and harmony that grounds the higher dimensions on Earth to an ever-widening circle, to more humans who are ready to be awakened to their true God-nature.

Glory be to you, O platinum Master of light, O platinum member of the angelic choir on this Earth plane, O platinum member of that club of spiritual mastery.

But where your club's membership differs from the existing exclusive platinum clubs and memberships on the Earth today is that it is inclusive. It wants to expand its membership. It wants to give platinum mastery to all and sundry. If they will have it, if they will work for it. And so the membership will expand over time. New chords will be struck. New overtones of light will resound as the pitch grows and as the music swells.

Let the platinum age begin anew. Let the platinum light of balance and harmony and unity fill the planet. And we will create heaven on Earth.

White—*Representations of Reality Revealed*

Sometimes when you are in a funk, when you are in a state of disarray, when all looks black or maybe even many shades of gray, that is when the purity of Source, the purity of Creator, the purity of the Universe is needed as incandescent white light that obliterates all and reconstitutes all in its over-lighting glory.

Consider if you will how a bird chirps when it is hungry and then flies when it is fulfilled. You, as a human, instead of chirping when you are in need, often express yourself in forms that are not as graceful. Perhaps you let fear and anger express itself as a kind of release of emotion, of sound, of action that can be harmful to others, until you get your way, until you are satisfied and sated.

So let us examine this particular human condition. We all, when put in the appropriate situation of need, of deprivation, can succumb to the earthly, human desire to assert, maim until it claims that which it desires. So let us embrace this human condition instead of denying it. Let us embrace this machine, this body, into which we have imbued our divine, white spiritual light. Let us know and acknowledge that our journey in this lifetime, as we experience a monumental Shift in consciousness, is about accepting our humanity, our animalistic self as we move more of our spiritual selves into this vehicle.

For, in order to fly, we must be grounded into the vehicle that maintains. We must be attuned to our moods. We must take responsibility for where life has taken us, for where actions have surprised us, and for where we have embraced shades of gray in hurting others, in order to satisfy ourselves. And as we do this, we are not validating or encouraging behavior that harms others. We are simply acknowledging that part of the human journey has been into the dark, into the void, and this is natural in a planet where there is free will, free choice.

So, just like a bird, you have sung your song, you have chirped in many ways, in many voices, across many lifetimes. Sometimes the song was joyous, sometimes the song was mournful, sometimes the song was wrathful. In any event, it was part of your journey, it was part of your evolution, and every step along the way was perfect, was exactly the way it was meant to be, and has taken you to where you are today.

So, as you now begin to explore the flight, the airy qualities that accompany the Shift, as you find yourself transformed into a white dove of peace and reconciliation, as you find yourself a harbinger of the Creator, and shifter of states of awareness and consciousness, you tap into the higher states of being, the higher states of awareness that take you far, give you a wider perspective.

For as you fly aloft, spreading your spiritual purity and absorbing your wider vision of what is down below, you know that as you continue through this incarnation, as you fulfill your mission of that which you came to fulfill in this lifetime, you will beckon to you the essence of the Earth, of humanity, of your body. You will land many times on this earth plane to feed, to nourish yourself and others, to share parts of your white dove self to those parts of humanity that are still in the process of transforming, of learning to fly.

Embrace and celebrate your duality. Embrace and celebrate your essence of Spirit and human. Divine and Earthly. You are the expression of everything rolled into one. And that is why, as you recognize who you really are, you find yourself in a white covering of feathers. For the color white encompasses all others in equal proportion. And so it is and always will be, across all dimensions and across all Universes.

And whenever you now stumble into the dark. Accept it, embrace it, and then transform yourself, and say out loud: "Let there be light". And away you will fly up high, as a white dove of nature, of spirit and of all.

Burnt Ochre—*Salaam*[29] *to The Glowing Eternal Being That You Are*

If you would like to taste the true grit of the Earth, to be part of the essence of Gaia, then flourish yourself with a cloak of burnt ochre.

Manifest it from the elements of the earth, the dust, the different compositions of yellows and browns and reds, until you make for yourself that composition that sways a bit here and there in hue, but gives an overall impression of earthiness, of smokiness, of a rich, reddish hue, what we call burnt ochre.

And it is burnt because it has absorbed the energies of the Sun that it rotates around. It has absorbed the energies of the Great cosmic Central Sun that beams energies to Earth via the portal of the Sun in our galaxy.

This burning, this bruleéing sensation, creates a rich, reddish hue, like the Earth's color in Sedona, in Harappa[30], or in a sunset or sunrise. And much like the crusty, burnt topping of a crème brulee, it adds that extra sense of excitement, for the burnt taste juxtaposed with the creamy sweetness of Gaia underneath allows you to appreciate the creaminess, the earthiness underneath even more.

So as you wrap your burnt ochre cloak around you, dear ones, you find that this burnished luster that glimmers and gloats in its magnificence around you, both connects you to your earthly body and its fineness, and at the same time in a sense aglows your inner soul, providing the outer crusting that makes your inner beauty even more delicate, more pristine, more evangelical[31].

For, in adding your earthly coat, in adding this red, burnt ochre around you, you pay homage to your physical body and its earthly composition. And you also acknowledge that you are providing the cover for something much more beautiful, much more evanescent underneath: your soul that is a reality for eternity.

And as your soul's special flavor is enhanced by its burnt ochre cloak, the sun's rays, as expressed and filtered through your cosmic crown and cosmic chakras flow out through the cloak and through the world, making the cloak even more burnt, even more reddish, even more burnished and beautiful.

And so you fuse the earthly composition of multicolored ochre with the god-like sun energies of yourself. And you express your mastery in being a spirit in a body, you express your superiority over all that is temporal. You assert your forever status, you sense of always having been, your sense of always going to be. For you are eternal. And you glow with a burning fever of excitement about yourself, about your god-self, for you are a creator of all there is. And you will always be.

Wisteria—*Pruning a Vine, Blooming Forever*

Up to a period of time the wisteria vine is acceptable. It is pretty, pink and violet and displays the colors and feelings of the higher vibrations. It spreads a sense of happiness and blooming across the board.

But when it goes too much across the board, takes up too much room, so that it starts clouding over the other trellises and windows and plants and harbingers of being that it is adorning, that is the time to say ok, have we had enough of the wisteria.

Similarly, dear ones, as you progress through your Spiritual awakening and journey to higher realms of remembering who you really are, you will find yourself often cultivating and blooming in the higher violet vibrations of the crown chakra, of connecting to Spirit.

But sometimes, and this is especially true when life goes awry, you sometimes get tired of staying in the vibration, of connecting, when the results are not what you desire, when things go out of balance, when things take over and cloud other windows and trellises and harbingers of being in your life.

This is when you which to sever your relationship for a while. This is when you wish to go out drinking or smoking or taking drugs, to escape the pain, the lack of fulfillment.

But we say to you that instead of trying to cut down the wisteria of your Spiritual growth and connection, instead of trying to dislodge it and take it apart, instead of trying to undo that which cannot be undone, simply accept the wisteria, once fully grown and awakened in you, as an essential and irremovable part of your life.

Once you have experienced the beauty, the lavender essence of the Creator, this beauty will take a hold of you with a violet embrace of the wisteria, never letting you go. For once you have tasted such beauty, you can never let it subside, never let it go.

And you might prune certain branches, take diversions outside of spirituality, and this is encouraged. But it is important to choose wisely.

A sense of disillusionment might point you towards drugs and bad company. A sense of illumination, of knowing that the Creator will help you manifest your desired reality in due course, as a co-creation, will lead you to happy diversions, such as sport, skiing, games, time spent loving and helping all the many loved ones in your family and among your friends, and even those who are strangers, if you are so moved to do so.

For, in seeking the happier diversions, you continue to believe and so you shine a wisteria brightness of violet beauty like a flashlight to others. And in so doing you attract your desired reality to you over time. You create your fantasy. You bloom in full Christ-consciousness glory.

And you might be a little pruned in that you might have shifted your focus from certain windows or trellises or harbingers of being your spiritual self, but eventually you return to your wisterian growth to higher levels and newer places.

For you are intrinsically spiritual at heart. You cannot help it. You are vineous energy seeking to grow and express violet beauty. And this is a universal truth.

Crimson—*Artifice, Shed Before, Becomes a Mantle of Higher Glory*

In olden times, the color crimson signified glory or disaster, depending on your perspective.

Glory if you were victorious, disaster if you succumbed. In either case, crimson blood would often flow, symbolizing the victory of the conquerors and the disaster of those vanquished.

In modern times, the blood still flows, unfortunately, and it still displays the self-same crimson color of glorious retribution.

For the ancient ways have not receded. The ancient wounds and hurts still drive the veiled man, who, lost in this third dimensional game, seeks a victory over his enemy, seeks to claim his pound of flesh from those who would oppose him, those who would stymie his desire to supercede, to vanquish.

And so, dear ones, you find that the bloody wars of death and retribution continue, whether in the Middle East, or in Pakistan, or in North Korea. The hot spots of the world are still lost in a crimson confusion of elemental desire to be the ones who are victorious, to be the ones who shed the blood and hence save their own skins, their own crimson beauty under the sheath of unscarred skin.

If you were to ask any of these conquistadors, these modern warriors of unending wars, what they are fighting for, they would tell you that they are fighting for their glory, for their honor, as symbolized by the crimson color of the blood they will shed. Whether the blood flows on their side or on the others will determine their moment of honor, of being the ascended victors, hailing from the ancestry of those who have been victorious before.

But we would like you, dear ones, to help these warriors see that a new version, a new shade of crimson is emerging in this rapidly changing world you are living in.

As you go through the Shift in Consciousness, there will be a time when a lot of the illusions fall away, when those who rabidly wish to shed the crimson blood of the enemy on the other side of an imaginary line will realize that the line does not exist and that the enemy is actually part of himself, a brother, a soul-friend playing this earthly game in the third dimension with him.

And when this realization comes into full force, sometime in the near future, the anger and malice will melt away in an explosion of tears and disbelief, just like a glacier melting under the full force of global warming. The tears will flow, washing away the crimson blood that has been shed in the name of false glory and false honor.

And those who shed tears and embrace their former enemies will create a cape of crimson glory around the new-found amity between all. This crimson cape will protect all in a meticulous embrace, making sure that such affronts to the soul inside never are perpetrated again. The cape will serve as a reminder of what has come before, and what will never be allowed by yourselves again.

And as you forgive yourself, for forgive yourself you must, as you travel forth into a new world of amity and loving and god-consciousness, your new crimson cape begins to reflect your new-found majestic glory of higher consciousness, reflecting the royal crimson capes of old, where the wise sages and kings expressed their singular mastery over their kingdoms in a blood-red color, reflecting their inner attunement to the pulse of all, to that which flows within themselves and within all.

Some call it crimson blood that binds us in our DNA. We call it our cosmic love for each other and for all creation.

Glory be to him who rises to this new-found glory of higher wisdom and attunement. And in this ascension of consciousness claims the crimson cape of knowledge and wisdom, and glorious love.

Mango—*Ripening the Sun-God Within*

In a pinch one wants to rush, to find the solution immediately. When there seems to be no exit, that is when we rush around frantically, looking for any door, any window that will take us out of our misery, out of our fearfulness, out of our sense of existential doom.

A happenstance that is often misconstrued is this very one of being caught in a trap, of being boxed in, of being crated, so to speak.

And we mention the word crated because that is how a mango might feel as it is being transported around the world in close quarters, tightly packed, so that others might enjoy the flavor it has to offer, in other parts of the world.

For your sense of confinement, your sense of being pressed in upon is part of a journey, part of your travels. You are on your way to finding the next port of call where you can shine your specific mango light, where others might not have experienced it before. And there is something specific in the crating process which ferments you, ripens you for this wider spreading of your taste, of your flavor, of your color.

In a sense, your particular skin changes color from an unripened green to a specific shade of mango yellow that is perfect for you. There are infinite varieties of beings, just as there are many types of mangoes, and many colors of mangoes, both in their skins as well as in their fleshy fruit inside. And so, as you ripen, in your inner crate of growth, and as you move forward to your next destination, your specific color is allowed to emerge, while in hibernation, while it is in darkness, in confinement. This allows you to let your unique flavor be without expecting it to be any specific shade of mango, any specific vibration.

For, if you were to simply move forward in your journey with the light of rational awareness and without the test of confinement, you would try to impose an expectation on your next step, you would try to make it be something you have been before.

And the whole point of the confinement, the crating, is to let yourself be that which you really are, that which you have not rationally known before as a human being, but that which you are as a universal being, in the higher dimensions.

So do not rush, dear ones, as you are confined in a crate of ripening, of maturation. Do not beat on the exterior boundaries, trying to break it open. Know that when you arrive at your destination, in perfect flow, with the timing of your destiny, you will find that portal to exit from in an easy slide to your next port of call, fully ripened, with an exquisite mango look that is unique and your particular flavor, with a particular taste and color of flesh to share with those you have chosen to journey to.

And as they now taste your fully ripened, wisened and delicious mango self, they understand the golden godly being that you are and have now chosen to bring into the earthly plane to share with others.

And they thank you for your courage in enduring the tests, the crating that allowed for your ripening, for your journey, so that you could bring this vibration in for the growth and amelioration of themselves and others who will experience you.

Parrot Green—*Mimicking and Spreading Joy, Healing Others along the Way*

In a sense when one is overcome with joy, with happiness, with the fulfillment of all one's dreams, one smiles and wants everyone to know.

We want everyone to know our sense of accomplishment; we want everyone to share our glory, our reaching of the heights of creation and absolution.

And so we share our sense of wealth and health and success with all and sundry. We call others up on the cellphone, we clamber up the stairs and scream out our good fortune at the top of our lungs, and ring the bells anywhere we can find them. We resonate the news, we spread it, we mimic it in many ways. And so we find ourselves becoming parrot-like, repeating the same word or concept many times, sometimes in annoying ways for others.

Reason goes out the window when we are successful. We cannot see the misery and unhappiness that might still exist in those around us. We ignore the baleful looks of those who seem to say: "Oh, please shut up. Must we hear more about how everything is going right in your life? Must we know how your dreams are coming true, when ours are still burdensome, heavy and difficult to imagine as a reality?" We *must* simply share our news and we go on chirping in a parrot-like fashion.

So, dear ones, know that as you simply flaunt your success and well-being and close yourself from the awareness and well-being of others, you in a sense create a separation between you and others. You create a seamless wall of parrot green, one that creates envy and malicious desires in others. It is a wall that might appear spring-like and beautiful to you, yet sickly and annoying to the one on the other side who finds that life is not as exciting, as promising, as it is for you.

Remember that in life, there are ups and downs. There are times when you will shout and repeat your good news from the rooftops and the rafters. There are times when you will be curled up in a ball of misery in the dark cave of desolation as you sort out your misfortunes and live within uncontainable fear. It is part of the ebb and flow of life.

So when you are gay, when you are happy, when you are achieving your dreams, we say to you that it is important to maintain a sense of humility. It is important to remain aware that there are others not as fortunate as yourself, not as abundant as yourself, not as full of themselves.

And so, an opportunity presents itself to you to transform yourself from a sickly parrot green that can be annoying in its sweet ripeness, it its insidious slalom of self-congratulation and delight.

For as you begin to acknowledge the misfortunes that others face, as you begin to realize that happiness is temporary, success is temporary, and that dark moments, unsuccessful moments, are as much part of this game as the lighter moments, you find yourself transforming into a new version of this parrot.

You find yourself transforming into a bird that speaks its truth only once, in words that are not repetitive, not mimicking and cloying, but pithy and wise and imbued with a sense of humility and a desire to share this abundance with others not as fortunate as you.

You become a more enlightened parrot, and you, in your more careful speed, in your new, higher vibrational green plumage, now attract others to you who want to learn about your success and who no longer feel threatened by you, no longer feel envious of you.

And you share your pearls of wisdom with them. And perhaps one or two or more might be inspired by your dashing heroism in claiming your life and your dreams and fulfilling your fantasy of success and happiness.

And perhaps they will resonate with a green healing and flower in the green glory of the plant kingdom. And eventually, via osmosis, they will be inspired to their own unique, individual success. They will transform into parrots themselves, successful, and ready to discuss their truth, their experience.

But remember to share this wisdom with them as well, for we do not want a mimicking, repetitive parrot green to permeate the world. A more refined sensibility, a more refined healing green that chooses its words carefully and let's its concepts stick very easily and heal as it does, finds expression as the new green, the new bird of love, spreading its pearls of wisdom in a pithy and generous way.

Taupe—*Ordinary to Extraordinary and Celestial*

Ordinarily, one would be confused when discussing the color taupe. It seems to define a sense of neutrality, but that neutrality is itself elusive. The color taupe can be seen as a dark shade of brown, it can be seen as a shade of gray, it can be seen as a shade of mauve. Its multiplicity of appearance makes it blend in, in a sense, to all that is. It is an expression of not standing out, of blending in.

So dear ones, we want you to consider that the color taupe, when you dwell on it, reminds you that often you simply try to blend into life, that often you simply try to go with the flow, and not make any waves. You like to be part of the community, and so you do not want to draw any attention to what you call your differences, but what we call your unique attributes and flavors.

For, dear one, you are a unique star of brightness, ready to be unfurled, ready to be unleashed unto the world. Your fire and desire, although tamed into a taupe of neutrality, by your childhood programming, by the sense of conformity that has been forced unto you by your community, is about to be ignited.

And so, imagine now a big finger of the Creator, shining bright and expressing that part of you that is already inside you, but ready to be ignited, touching your heart chakra and sparking alight that divine aspect of you that you have tried to hide for so long.

And as the Creator's expression and touch rekindles a birth of your divine self, your neutrality, your taupian sense of "I will hide myself because I want to belong" begins to evaporate, begins to melt away.

And you find that you are actually comprised of multiple colors and vibrations, many of the colors of the rainbow, and many colors that cannot even be perceived on this Earth plane.

Notice your many colors and rejoice. Throw your taupe cloak away and be the multi-colored being you were meant to be.

Breathe deep and exhale brightly, spreading your colors far and wide. And like a paintbrush, your colors begin to override the taupian neutrality of others, awakening in them their own individual colors, their own individual inner light.

Breath deep again, dear ones, holding onto the notion of taupe for those that need it at appropriate times—like the mole when it needs to hide, and has not been emancipated, like that unawakened, unconscious soul that is trying to ignore the growing light of his or her Creator self as the Shift proceeds in an exponential fashion. And be compassionate for the choices that some make to hold onto their taupian neutrality, their reluctance to let go of conformity.

But let yourself transcend any limitations and come into full resplendent view.

Red Rose—*Creating A Rose Garden of Love on Earth*

Upon a crimson night, a crimson night of romance and ardor, as your heart beats in a red hot fury of pulsating blood, and the crimson sunset heralds the start of an ardor and romance much anticipated, much desired, you hold in your hand a beautiful red rose, the ultimate symbol of the purity of your love.

This rose of ancient wisdom and high frequency emits from its many-folded leaves a hum of insistence and desistance.

It emits your note, your hum of pure desire to express, to love and share the inner beauty that you have hidden for so long. For you are ready now, dear one, to share with the world that part of your crepuscular, heavenly glory that you were afraid to show before; afraid, for you had wondered: "Will I get trampled? Will I be cut short, trimmed, pruned, besmirched?"

And what has changed now that has allowed you to step forward on this wondrous night of the Creator's beauty and offer your delicacy of red rosiness, your ethereal, eternal hum and tone to others and share your love?

The Shift, dear one, which is occurring now and rapidly increasing its pace, is allowing a slackening and lifting of the veils. And, as this takes place, you are beginning to glean glimpses of the higher realms, of the higher dimensions.

And these glimpses are dropping down holy water into your holy, sacred heart chakra, nourishing the red rose buds of crimson glory and arduous endeavor and boundless love that have been securely hidden in the past with fear, with disappointment, with an expectation of lack.

The gardener has found you and you are ready to be brought back to life, to be resuscitated into your loving, ethereal self that is not afraid to give, to share, to emit your hum.

For the Shift is coming, and for those who allow their red roses to bloom, for those who let this wonderful high frequency flower of unconditional love emit their unique hum, there is a Paradise ahead.

This is an earthly paradise, dear ones. One where you recognize your divine, incorruptible essence while still in human embodiment. One where you fully anchor in your god-like self into a body that changes to higher frequencies itself to accommodate the larger spirit that will be inhabiting it.

And so your proffer your red rose of purity and unconditional love now to others. You wish to help them bloom themselves, help them discover their own red rose. And in your desire to garden the others and help them take advantage of the tremendous opportunities for soul growth offered by the Shift, you move your rose into the earth, grounding it and creating a rose bush, one that blooms in universal beauty.

And you start a garden in this Earth, in this reality, providing the pathway for others to create their own bushes, with their own individual hums adjacent to yours, in the growing community garden of heaven on Earth.

And, as more and more humans reclaim their god-self and spread unconditional love to all others, spreading their rose bushes together all across this planet, we will move to a higher level of consciousness, a higher level of being.

And those who do not wish to partake of the joyous beauty of the higher dimensions will be allowed to continue their soul adventure on another planet, another 3rd dimension that suits their vibration.

For we of the red rose frequency choose light and love and community. And with an ardor that is head-spinning in its integrity and purity we birth the new earth, with a new garden of Eden right here, right now, as part of the Shift to the 5th dimension of reality.

Welcome home!

Silver—*Bursting into the New You*

A burst of silver energy explodes into your space. You feel as if you are in another dimension, another aspect of reality. Your mind is glowing with embers of moonlight, of pieces of energy that seem foreign, from far off lands, from the mystical areas of Avalon and Camelot.

And indeed, dear ones, silver is the energy of alchemy, of transmuting magically what is dross, what must be released, into a new frequency, a frequency of love, of no inhibitions, of being who you really are: a magician, a modern-day Merlin.

So, imagine if you will, silver energy pouring out of your heart chakra, reflecting the specific energies of your magical talents, and see this energy floating and spiraling across your space, across your aura.

See yourself spinning around, like a top, within this silver energy, until you find yourself in a room, room of intention and dissolution. There are silver mirrors coating all the walls and you find images of yourself reflected and refracted back to you in silvery light

Set your intention now to claim your inner magician, to claim you inner Merlin, and let that which is not part of you, that which is the analyzer, the programming of the 3rd dimension, dissolve from your space.

See the non-silver energies, the different colors you do not need, now streaming out of your body to all the different silver mirrors, which absorb, transmute and dissolve back to the Universe that which you are moving on from.

Take a deep breath, dear one, for you are climbing up the ladder of ascension. You are saying hello to and becoming that which you already are: a master magician.

Hail to thee and claim the beast within which is to be unleashed. And this is not the Biblical fear-based beast to be feared.

This is your inner lion, your inner sun, your inner silver that is about to express its silvery magical moonlight to the world. Say aloud: Aloha, mahola, masa no karma. And be free.

Crown Chakra
Ash Tree—Rekindling the Inner Crown

Know that when a phoenix rises from the ashes, it is rekindling itself. It is not so much a rebirth as a redefinition, a refiring of self. For it is in the new dispensation of the new consciousness that is accelerating around your Earth that you will begin to understand that you, too, in your own way will go through crises, will be reduced to ashes, so to speak, and will be refiring yourself into a new, fully super-charged human, ready for the new dispensation.

You will have several new strands of DNA that will come forth over time in this new, rekindled you. You will be able to fight disease and viruses more easily. You will be able to regrow and regenerate not only your inner phoenix, but your bone marrow, your cells, your atoms, your organs. You will become a super human for the new millennium.

And so you will begin to embody that ancient and magical tree know as the Ash. You will be strong and sturdy, and you will reach to the heavens in your new strength, your new superhuman abilities, showing that the human form is an expression of Spirit, of the Creator, of all that is.

As you sprout new branches and new leaves in this rekindled self, full of strength and vigor, full of knowledge that is quantum and divine, you will begin to grow a fiery gold color within your crown chakra. For your crown will be spilling over with the golden light of the golden sun, the Great Central Sun from whence you came.

As you channel this light through your crown chakra into your body you will emit high frequencies of knowledge and light to all, sending messages and alighting the inner Sun in all those around you who are ready to receive the message of their inner divine self.

And your crown chakra will transform itself into the shape of a kingly crown, for you are all kings, you are all a part of the God, of the Great Central Sun, and you will be shining your glory to all and sundry with pride, claiming your birthright as a Spirit with infinite abilities and boundless creativity and unconditional love for all.

And for those who get alighted by your rekindled self, your God-fired crown of self acceptance and self-regeneration, they will see in your ash-like strength and superhuman ability a new channel with which to understand themselves. They will find a frequency on their dial of possibilities that had previously been invisible to them.

No longer will they wait for the Ash Wednesdays of their religions to anoint themselves with the markings of atonement and repentance, willing themselves into limitation, into a subjugated, fearful sense of self.

No, they will now find in your rekindled light a special show, a special spectacle of celebration that allows them to take off the disguise, the costume of limitation that duality had imposed on them.

They will burn up the limitations into ashes, and will arise anew, over time, rekindled, superhuman, quantum, and kingly, firing golden crowns within, and alighting more around them to rise up from the ashes.

And so it goes.

Chapter 9
Geometric Flowerings of Consciousness

Lily—*Heartfelt Purity*

According to Matthew[32], the Lily is a symbol of purity[33], of the Madonna, of Christian essence.

Its six leaves form a Star of David, a nascent star tetrahedron[34], waiting to explode into the hearts of those who smell it and convey them, through the purity of love, to the higher dimensions of existence.

We say unto you that a lily is to be grown and nurtured in your heart to grow and connect to others at a level of compassion, of acceptance and of non-judgment.

Imagine an etheric white lily in front of you now, its six petals hinting at the star tetrahedron it will create around your heart chakra, which, when it spins, will melt away all of your culturally programmed judgments.

Smell the essence of this healing lily, and bring it in now, into your heart, into your heart chakra.

Feel it spinning, churning, inside your heart, releasing the dross, the judgments about those who are different from you, those who are disadvantaged, those who are disabled. Release your cultural programming now as the lily spins its magic.

Rise in your newly found purity into a steeple of wisdom, of compassion, of ease and of heartfelt love.

Let your lily bloom and you will soon become the **Christed Being** that all of humanity is becoming as they move closer to a Shift of consciousness to the **Christ Consciousness**, to the grid of love that has been anchored around your planet[35].

Reach for the stars not in the sky, but in your heart, for the lily inside represents the star that is you, as it spins the star tetrahedron.

Water Lily—*Rebirthing the Sun-God Within*

In the inner wisdom and inner sanctum of Nature, much is understood and created anew every day, as the first buds of light come and strike away the blighted night every morning, revealing with the rays of the rising sun those creative drops of ethereality[36] that form rainbows of delight for all to see the light of the new days with the golden rays that come forth from the diurnal rising of the Ra, the Sun-God of old.

And so it is that the water-lily, ancient and blue, known well since ancient Egyptian times, would rise anew every morning, birthing itself again and again from the depths of the creative power of Mother Nature, or Gaia, coming forth from the embryonic waters of life, to the surface of the Earth, bringing with it the harbingers of a new dawning, its blue petals feeding the sleeping young Ra, rising now anew with the fresh creations of water and earth, breathing the air, to light with golden fire the birth of a new day[37].

And it is in the phyllotaxis[38] of the spiral of the growth of this sacred blue water lily from the core of creation to be born anew into the fires of heat and regeneration, that one discerns the precise geometry of Nature, the **Fibonacci**[39] sequence of the **golden mean**[40], of that perfect proportion that allows this flower to bloom anew each day in ratios of 5s, 8s, 13s and 21s, spiraling into existence, through the earth and the water, and birthing anew with a burst of fresh air, the breathing of the life of creation manifested into a 3rd dimensional reality.

And so it is that just as Ra, the Sun-God, the rising Sun who was birthed anew through the elements of earth, water, and air every day, spiraled up into a manifestation of fiery expression and warmth, so it is that you too chose to become incarnated in your body on Earth, your body composed of the elements of earth and water, breathing in the air of your planet, so that you could birth anew the golden light of ascension that is coming your way very quickly.

For you are about to rise again, O Reader, into a new-born Ra as you claim your golden light and birth anew the fiery essence of self that is the divine fire of your Spirit within.

And, as you blaze forth into the higher expressions of yourself, you spiral up to a higher dimensional expression, to a higher blueprint of expressing your destiny, as you grow in the perfect golden ratio of Self.

O Atman of new, O water lily of old, your blue water lily of certainty births and rebirths a golden child of the New Age.

And, so, you father the consciousness of the new livelihood of humanity and you rise into your role as leader and god and creator at this important time of change, for all those who will follow in your footsteps as you lay the foundations of a new day that is dawning for humanity, as the Shift in consciousness proceeds.

Dandelion—*Parachuting into a New Beginning*

When you pick a dandelion flower you notice its beauty, its flowering essence, expressing the effervescent joy and ebullient "lion's tooth" intrinsic within its nature, as it smiles to you with its *"dent de lion"*[41].

It is preparing you, with love, for the journey you have been taking in this lifetime as a soul, journeying into the far reaches of 3rd dimensional experience, as you parachute yourself into this reality from the starlight and the lion's strength from which you flowered.

And so it is, that as you observe the many dandelions that are created in the garden of nature, expressing rosettes of fiery, and golden beauty, you also notice that some, in the full flowering and creation of themselves, are then ready to explore, to bounce anew into new realms of journeying and of existence, just as you have.

And you notice the flowers transforming into glistening parachute balls, with each spoke expressing its lattice-like geometry, a fine spreading out of silvery webs and strands, just like the strands of mitochondria within your DNA.

And each spoke connects with the other, creating a web, a geometry that represents the unity of this pattern, this flowering that is about to be dispersed, freed to explore many new adventures, before it eventually flowers again into the lion's tooth from whence it came.[42]

And we suggest to you that this parachute ball of explosion and implosion, this unity of creation that allows for adventure and a revergence of the essence of self-flowering, we suggest to you that this ball is like the geodesic dome[43] that surrounds your planet, creating a grid of support around you, representing the light of unity from whence you came before you dispersed from your soul family to many Creator games, including this Earthly 3rd dimensional game of duality.

And this geodesic dome is helping humanity ascend into a new vibration that is united, that is filled with community, as each of the stars within the parachute that once parachuted to different cultures and different lifetimes are reunited once again with the golden Christed grid of light that, as a geodesic dome, is alighting the ways for a reemergence of a united humanity, connected once again, not only by the mitochondria within the cells of their own bodies, but connected also by new mitochondria, ethereal mitochondria, that are being formed between evolving and ascending humans as telepathic waves of communication, creating geodesic domes of connections on the ascending Earth plane, mirroring the grids of ascension above the planet.

So celebrate your journey, your dispersal, your parachuting into the realms of experience and growth, for the geodesic dome is growing once again to allow you to reconnect, to find a new flowering of yourself, so that you find yourselves on a New Earth that is verdant and green and you all bloom in harmony, with the strength of lions, smiling and showing your teeth with love, spreading yellow and golden colors and light in the field of verdure you now adorn.

Squash Blossoms—_Star Blossoming Into Ascension_

Into the frying pan you might sauteé some squash blossoms, and smell the spreading warmth of the star-like flower that provides fruit for your hearth.

And this flower, in its own edibility, represents the complete package of service that each star seed, each soul who has come to Earth for this game of duality, expresses in living lives in a 3rd dimensional existence; those who have chosen to come forward at this time of the Shift, so that all can be helped to transition to a higher vibrational reality.

And so it is that the squash blossom, that flower of the squash vegetable, represents, in its geometric structure, the 5 petals that are characteristic of flowers that bear fruit, so to speak, for their 5 petals represent the pentagon, the regeneration of life through the offering of nurturing and sustenance that regenerates the star within each human.

And so, the pentagon of the flower becomes inscribed with the pentagram, the 5-pointed star within, heralding the arrival of the star-seeds' self-awareness of self as the star within recognizes the star patterns within nature.[44]

So, as you sauteé your squash blossoms in your frying pan, and as they sizzle, notice that you, the flower of life, the star seed from whence you incarnated into your current body, also are sizzling now at this time of the Shift as the energies and vibrations of change intensify.

But how you respond to this sizzling is really your choice. You can choose to be excited and express the ebullience of being transformed in taste into the holder of a cooked flower that will give new tastes to humanity, providing vessels for new light waves to be radiated through you as human crystals, and melding the light of the Creator, of all, of Unity, into the community, as you spread part of your transmitted light to all, as they digest the light of the vessel of the star that came to help humanity ascend.

Or, you can choose to see the sizzling and the frying as a negation of your inner self, of a movement to a catastrophic ending as the winds of change cause calamity all around you, as you buy into the media stories of the 2012 end of days dramas.

Well, if you choose to go down this road, my dear ones, you will become too scared to really want to change at all. You will hold on fast to the edge of the pan, not wanting to transform. And so the buds of your leaves will stay closed. They will not unfurl to reveal the star patterns within. And you might find yourself exiting this Earth reality, for you will not be choosing to ascend.

So our message to you today is to take a deep breath when you find life sizzling all around you, to notice the 5-fold symmetry of all of nature, whether it exists in flowers, in the sequence of the Fibonacci numbers of growth, in the 5 fingers and toes of your hands and feet, in the five extremities branching from your torso, as familiarized by Leonardo da Vinci in his famous painting of man[45], or in the star pattern that is knitted into the core of your very sacred heart.

And, as you do this, as you connect with the regeneration and growth that is at the core, at the heart of all creation, you will understand that in choosing a vibration of adventure as you go through the next few years of change, you will allow for a most magical transformation, as from the frying pan you find yourself imbibed and transformed into a new assimilated being, one that has assimilated many aspects of its multidimensional and higher self, one that is fully connected with the star-qualities of the Creator, for the star already exists within.

It is the opening of this flower, it is the offering of your smell and unique flavor as an act of service, that will allow you to ascend in earnest.

Shamrock—*Understanding the Trinity Within*

When a trefoil is examined, whether within the context of a three-leaved clover, or shamrock, or within the context of a tight-fitting knot, there is a perfect symmetry in the trinity that is evoked; there is a balancing, a harmony, a sense of ease.

And so it is that as you contemplate the beautiful symmetry of the three-leaved shamrock you understand the importance of the number 3 in the Universe.

The trinity is at the very core of creation. For just as there is a God/Goddess, or Supreme Being that created all, that balanced all, this Supreme being has 3 aspects to it.

And we wish to caution you here that we are not giving you a teaching on Christianity. We are simply allowing you to explore the trinity within, to open yourself up to the concept that just as a triangle is the most stable structure for construction, providing a foundation for edifices, so it is that the number 3 is the source of Universal Creation.

The Supreme Being can be understood as being a Parent figure, one that generates, via creation, aspects of itself for further exploration and understanding. And then there is the child figure, the actual manifestation of that Creation in the form that separates from the Father to actually create new vistas and Universes, to see what it is that can be created within the cosmos of all there is. And then there is the energy of Spirit, the energy of the raw power of the Elohims and Angels that provide the fire-power, the raw Spirit of creation to allow the Child energy to play with the building blocks of all there is. And this energy of Spirit, which we call here the Shekina energy of all there is, is somewhat analogous to the Christian concept of the Holy Spirit, but we wish to separate our characterization of the Shekina creative force as separate of the straitjacket of religiosity imposed by your 3rd dimensional linear creations.

So, as you contemplate your shamrock, know that you have all three aspects of the Supreme Being already within you and this shamrock symbolizes this back to you. You, as an aspect of Spirit, are yourself a Supreme Being for you, in your highest multidimensional existence, already are connected to and are a part of the Creator.

And so, on this Earth, you, as your own Supreme Being, can create anew your reality, your life, and each creation. Whether it is a piece of art, a construction, an experience, a job or a relationship, it is a manifestation of your Creator Self, for you have given birth to a child which reflects your very instrinsic nature of creating something anew and experiencing it.

And the Shekina energy that you employ to create a creation which makes you laugh and be happy, is the simple, fundamental joy of the Spirit of creation, of the fire that burns deep within to enjoy every experience, to be curious about what comes your way, and absorb the opportunities it provides for learning.

And as a Creator, as a Supreme Being on this Earth plane, you create every aspect of your reality. And this includes all the negative and debilitating experiences, my dear ones. For you have been led to believe, by the cultural programming within your space that all the bad things that happen to you are because you have been bad, and so you make yourself into a victim.

It is time now, dear ones, as this Shift in Consciousness for the planet proceeds, for you to give up this victim consciousness and recognize that *you* created each misadventure for you transformed the Shekina energy of joy, curiosity and abundance into the creative energy of sadness, fear, and debilitation, leading you to experiences that reinforced these notions for you.

So use your shamrock now to give you inspiration that you can indeed transform your life. Pick three words that you would like to imbue your Shekina energy with, three words that empower the raw power of Spirit within you to create the new aspects of your future reality, to create the children, the progeny of your future existence.

Might we suggest some of the following words: abundance, gratefulness, adventure, curiosity, joy, alacrity, wisdom, sanctity, truth, integrity, teacher, lover, embracer, beholder of all there is. These are only a few examples, but pick any 3 of these words, or any others that fill your heart with the joy of a better future that you create and are not controlled by.

And let these 3 words fall into place into each one of the three leaves of your shamrock. Now connect up these words with imaginary lines, forming a triangle of stability that will form a foundation for your future ascension into the higher aspects of your multidimensional Creator self.

And then place this shamrock upon your heart, letting the trefoil of its design create a trefoil now of knowledge and certainty that connects with the three-fold flame of your Supreme Being that lies within your heart chakra, connecting your external reality, through this symbol of the Shamrock to the trinity-Creator truth that already burns bright within the recesses of the core of your spiritual being.

And this trefoil, this vibration of sounds now knots your external reality to your internal infinity forming a union that embraces your trinity.

And so you allow your experience of yourself to move towards the trinitized Supreme Being that you already are.

Sunflower—*Unfolding Geometrically Into Your Glorious Golden Potential*

Just a sunflower head's spiral makes you want to reach for the stars, to climb up your very own ladder of ascension, so it is that today we wish to enlighten you with information about how it is that the sunflower's sun disc, within its very center, can attune you to the notions and ratios of the fabrics of energy that make up your very being, that provide you with the tuning, so to speak, to let you rise and resurrect yourself from the ashes of the lower vibrations of yourself, that you are rapidly leaving behind, as you choose the path of ascension.

As we have already introduced the Fibonnaci sequence of numbers to you, in our description of the phyllotaxis of growth regarding the water lily, we will now show you a fundamental application of another part of the spiral of Fibonacci growth, that creates a logarithmic spiral of creation, with a golden mean, creating a ratio of unfolding the golden flower within you, as you reach up towards the great Central Sun that is the Supreme Being and alight it to the sparks of the inner divine design that are within you, as you begin to align your inner sun in spirals of the golden mean, to logarithmic ratios of attunement, connection and growth.

If you observe the sunflower's head, you will notice that it is made up of clockwise and counter-clockwise spirals, and that the ratio of numbers of seeds in each spiral is a sequence from the Fibonnaci series, for example, 34 and 55, and then 89 and 144 are also possibilities. And if this Earth allowed for even larger and bigger sunflowers, which it soon will, you will see developing sunflowers with spiral heads that go further in the Fibonacci sequence: 233 and 377, and so on.

The point is this: that just as the sunflower is known to unveil itself in a spiraling form, so it is that you, too, must unveil yourself to the ratios of the golden mean and let yourself connect in harmony to the laws of divine light, divine truth and divine wisdom in order to grow yourself, and to absorb the rays of the Sun.

And as you allow yourself to do this, you allow for the spiral of ascension to take root within your frame, allowing you to ride the waves of ascension energy that are now coming to your planet, as the planetary ascension proceeds apace. And so you release the karma from before and move from a circle of playing out the same patterns again and again to a spiraling movement up the frequencies of being

And the sunflower, as a bud, instinctively follows the movement of the Sun from east to west as it grows, knowing that this source of divine light and divine unfolding is the basis for its most beautiful and glorious flowering.

And so, you too, must connect with the Sun of cosmic light, the Supreme Being of insight that lives in the higher dimensions to allow for your own beautiful and glorious flowering, to unveil and unfold the true beauty within, that has always been.

And to do this, you meditate and imagine that you are spiraling up to connect with the higher aspects of yourself that lives in many dimensions. And as you do this, you create a resonance with aspects of yourself in higher dimensions, in ratios that are multiples of and expressions of the Fibonacci sequence, allowing for higher octaves of yourself to connect with you and deliver you the information you need that is perfect for you to help you move forward in a way that is perfect for your inner divine design of spiraling into the higher aspects of yourself as the Shift of consciousness unfolds.

And as you do this, you notice that the octaves that you are resonating with are themselves multiples of the number 8, which in its typographic representation, represents the sign of infinity, the sign of absolution, and of all there is.

And so, as you yourself connect with the ratios of Fibonacci sequences to the higher octaves of yourself, and you resonate with these aspects of yourself, as you allow yourself to become attuned to the higher parts of divinity that you yourself already are, you find yourself becoming a part of that infinity and you begin the spiral dance of ascension into the light of the new being that is more expanded, more fulfilled.

And as the Earth itself ascends, you will be able to explore higher and higher octaves of yourself, and just as the sunflower might develop larger flower heads with higher ratios of the Fibonacci sequence, so, too, might you unveil larger versions of yourself, not by leaving the planet, but by bringing them into your body, into your rooted self with the higher frequencies of the ascending Earth, allowing yourself to become a larger flower in your current incarnation.

And with your beauty, and your geometric expansion into the Golden ratios of higher love, light and wisdom, you will call to you the friends and honeybees who will create many opportunities and serendipitous events for you, allowing you to manifest your most glorious inner divine design with the assertion of the Sun God that you yourself are on the Earth plane, as you anchor in the golden light of higher knowledge and love with the golden ratios of spiraling ascension.

We share these truths with you to encourage you to admire the beauty within yourself, and also to remind you that the numbers and ratios of golden growth are natural and part of any organism that wishes to align with the sun and grow into higher aspects of itself.

Just like the sunflower, you already know how to grow and to become beautiful. Just let yourself surrender and connect to the divine. And let more of your inner beauty unfold.

Chapter 10
The Fruits of Ascension

Ananas—*Sprightly Ascension into the Helical Construction of Fiery Red Group Alignments of Higher Vibrational Reality*

In the overall structure of the pineapple, also known as the ananas, is the helical arrangement of individual flowers that find a way to connect with each other, to share individual fruits that coalesce into the heavenly manna of bromelein and protease-laced fruit that provides the God-given natural activants for stimulating your bodies and taking them to new heights of attunement and absolution.

And so it is that you, too, as you find yourself growing spiritually, not only through the knowledge you have gained and the pieces of nascent wisdom that have been activated in your frame through the words of Spirit you have been aligned with during the course of this book, but also through all the individual work and experience you do and claim in your everyday reality, whether it is through prayer, meditation, yoga or simply in communing with and helping another Spirit in a human body, you find that you, too, are connecting with the other flowers of Spirit who are human, and you, too, want to coalesce in a Spiritual community that finds a helical, strong and robust casing for the catalysts for growth for all that come through the community of the shared fruits of the group ananas that you are surely and steadily becoming as the Shift in consciousness proceeds apace.

And, if you compare your growth and coming together with others, with the mathematical arrangement of the ananas itself, you will discover that divine timing, in terms of the ratios of connection and reconnection with others means that even if the connections have not always flown by smoothly, even if you have felt frustrated at times because you expected different outcomes, it has been because it is the perfect Fibonacci arrangement that is being arranged for you and for your human community, one that allows for the helical arrangement of growth that is spiracular and heralds and presages the arrival of the New Age of Enlightenment.

We refer, of course, to the helical structure of the ananas where the fruits are arranged in patterns of 8 in one direction and 13 in the other, conforming to the ratios of Fibonnaci accretion, the basis not only of spiracular growth, but growth, within these series of ratios that confirm and adhere to the Golden Mean and ratio of phi that is the stamp of the Divine Will of the Creator for this local Universe that you inhabit.

And so it is that you will find the ratios of connection, as they align more directly with the Will of the Creator's plan for the Shift in Consciousness, heralded, but not specifically pinned down to the Winter Solstice 2012 date much hyped in your media-crazy world, will give you new opportunities to reconnect and find that helical structure of arrangement with the tufted connections that fit in with the tufted connections of other human flowers, as you all align to the overall pattern of the Shift, to the higher vibrations of light and the 4th and 5th dimensional reality that is rapidly coming your way as Gaia ascends, as the alignment of this Milky Way Galaxy to the Universal center of your local Universe and the alignment of your solar system to the Milky Way Galactic Center itself, allows for the creation and dissemination of the photon waves of light that represent the Divine Will of the Creator from the highest of the high, aligning you now, with divine timing, and with the divine phi ratios of the light that allow you to create a community of the higher 4th and 5th dimensions of light with those intrepid Spirits in human bodies who choose to wake up and construct this new helical, spiracular community with you.

And the ananas that you will create together of the beauteous enzyme-rich, golden-ratio trussed community of the new Age of enlightenment will be blessed by the Divine insight and potentials for accelerated growth embedded within the photon light band that your Earth and galaxy are now entering as an opportunity to align with the Throne of divine righteousness and Will of the Creator.

For you are all divine, you are all aspects of the Creator, and you all originally were one, choosing to divide and subdivide for experience and for service. And now, as you coalesce with love, divine insight and awakening into a new Age of Enlightenment which is rapidly dawning, you will find that your ananas of golden proportions, constructed within the divine timing of the alignment of the heavens for this evolution of Spirit in human form to its next octave of experience, turns into a fiery red color of divine insight and the will and righteous knowledge of divine love, divine light and divine wisdom, as your reclaim your Godly self and align with higher aspects of yourself that become more readily available to you as you experience the higher vibrations of light, in golden proportionate helical alignment, that the Shift in consciousness is rapidly affording you.

And so your group Earthly ananas encases you in a fiery red casing of beauty and grandiose wonder. If you have not seen the beauty of the red pineapple, we encourage you to gaze at a picture of this wondrous fruit. Know that as you encase yourself and your community in this higher red vibration of the casings and support of the divine light of the Creator God self you are rapidly becoming, you find nourishment as a community of vibrant connections.

It is no longer about being fruit, like the regular pineapple, which is available and delicious for the individual's growth through its enzyme-rich forms of reconnections and activations. You are now already connecting in new ways with your community in your vibrant red color of the divine will of the Supreme Being.

And as you get activated by the photon rays of absolution and dissolution of all that you are not, your new red ananas of love, joy and divine communion with each other and also with all there is means that your fruit is communal, to be shared with all by simply being. It is no longer about plucking the fruit and tasting its gifts for growth. You are already grown into a higher vibration of communal understanding. And this understanding is in itself its own fruit of fiery red communion, reflecting the divine insight and wisdom that is the hallmark of spiritual growth into the higher realms.

And so your red ananas becomes an emblem, a coronation of sort of your own kingly self. For this fruit is not often eaten. It is grown for it beauty, for its vibrations of higher divine insight and delight. And so we suggest to you that with this ascension into the Age of Enlightenment and group communal understandings, you will no longer be searching for individual paths of growth exclusively. You will have, as you partake and contribute to this red, fiery ananas, the divine understanding of the higher geometric ratios and symbols of spiritual connection that crown and coronate your emblemic red ananas shell, crowned literally by the trusses of divine leaves of ascension that thrust out of the head of your group, ascended red ananas.

Smile and know you are about to transform yourself and your world. And it will be a most wonderful, bounteous and amazing creation of the fiery red vibration of Spirit that reflects the divine will burning bright inside the sacred hearts of each one of you.

Pomegranate—*Trinitizing the Self into Spherical Unity*

Overall, a pomegranate is a mysterious fruit. It unveils a tapestry of red ruby pearls within, sheathed within a tripartite division of the levels of initiation that represent the merging of the soul with aspects of its Higher Self.

For, when the soul exists in an earthly incarnation, it feels severed, incomplete, separate from Spirit and from the rest of humanity. It feels as if the daily routine and daily grind of it all can make or break existence, and so takes every experience in life very seriously.

And, in the higher realms, the soul exists as part of a group consciousness, part of a tripartite expression of the Father/Mother God that is the Source of all there is, part of the Creator Son energy that came forth to manifest the creations of manifested universes and galaxies, and part of the Spirit of Spirit, that raw, creative, fiery energy that through many energetic building blocks that we call the Rays of Creation, helps manifest the visions of the Creator Sons that help Source experience and know itself in its many myriad expressions.

And so it is that the pomegranate, although each shell of the tripartite division is uniquely structured with the symmetrical arrangement of the red ruby pearls or arils of pomegranate oxidative healthfulness and fruitfulness that define this most abundantly healthy fruit, it is within the overall construction and alignment of the tripartite division of the trefoil of this fruit within the sphere of the outer casing of the membrane of this oxidative palliative and elixir that the true beauty and ability to manifest is to be found.

For the outer spherical casing of the fruit provides it with the membrane and protection to grow the red ruby arils within. It is the unity of the sphere that allows the individual seedlings to grow within. And as they come together, in the format of a pomegranate, the result is delicious, nourishing and fertile.

And so it is that when you break open the fruit, harvest the arils, and eat the juice and manna of this fiery red expression of Trinity energy, you care not from which part of the casings the juice comes from. You care not if the fruit is from the top half of the fruit or the bottom right. It all tastes all right to you, and that is indeed the vibration of unity.

And so, as you sometimes feel severed from Source as you go about your daily life, as you sometimes wonder why specific incidents are coming your way, as you wonder about the lack of manifestation in your life for what you truly desire, we suggest to you that you enlarge your perspective from that of separation to the overall Trinity of the construction of your experience to the Higher aspects of yourself that has planned your experiences, with a specific purpose.

And that purpose is to keep you aligned with your divine blueprint, to grow in your spiritual path, so that you can move to higher vibrations of yourself, that recognize group consciousness, that recognize that all of humanity is not separate, but from the same original pomegranate of Source that divided to experience many games, including this Earth game of free will, where many mutations such as fear, anger, envy and other lower vibrational thoughts and emotional forms have been allowed to be created to examine them, and eventually to transmute them.

For, as the Shift in consciousness continues apace, those who do not wish to accept these truths, those who do not see themselves as part of a larger whole will find it harder and harder to make sense of the events that come their way.

It is when they recognize that they are shiny red ruby arils that are part of an overall mosaic, a tapestry of connections with other souls and beings, and that it is in the collective community of working together and creating a new Earth filled with the vibrations of joy, love, candor, and every form of higher humanity that you can imagine, that they free themselves from the localized view of fear patterns of "poor me" and move into the higher connected forms of understanding that all of humanity is to be savored and nourished, and, in so doing, they connect with the Trinity of understandings within, merging with the Source, the Creator Son and the raw fire of Spirit within.

And, in so doing this, they create the beautiful red and pink outer casing of the ruby pomegranate around themselves and around the world, weaving a new understanding of a joint destiny that aligns with divine community and the higher aspirations of all, for in the ascension, you will be talking to each other telepathically and getting perspectives from your Higher Selves that shed new light on everyday experiences, and this will allow you to newly create the pomegranate of the New Earth that, in its nourishing oxidative power, will nourish not only each one of you, but all of humanity.

Glow inside with the pride of the pomegranate, for you embody the fiery Spirit of Spirit within your frame. That is how you were created. Believe in your creative fires within, and you will transform your life and your world, in harmony, and in community.

Star Fruit—*Revering the Self as the Divine Image of Infinity*

Every time we want to feel good we imagine ourselves receiving a star, for a star pattern as an archetype has always represented the achievement of superlative mastery, of that connection to the divine superman and atman that we ascribe to God and that we actually already are.

When you were a child in kindergarten, did you not receive stars on your work from the teacher to indicate that you had done well? And were you not made extra happy to get a gold star? For golden light and the golden frequency is what you identify with deep down within. And it is a golden star archetype that you are reclaiming for yourself as you grow in your own frequencies of light and affirmation and approbation, allowing for the unfurling of your own inner star. For you have always been a star inhabiting a human body, and instead of waiting to find that affirmation from an external teacher or boss or partner to reward you with a star of approval, we suggest that you find the star within to crown and cherish yourself with the anointment of the golden recognition of your inherently divine self.

And, so, it is that the star fruit is emblematic of the growing, unfurling mastery and divine design that is the central core of every divine creation of the Creator, including your human body. For, as we have referenced the Fibonnaci sequence of numbers, the phi ratio and the phyllotaxis of spiracular formation in a golden spiral in other pieces, we wish at this point to acquaint you with the central geometry of the 5-pointed star and it's connection to infinity, current reality and star-affirming neutrality.

The star shape is in itself perfectly symmetrical, its five points creating triangles of phi proportion, and the lines of the star crossing always in relation to the phi ratio, always finding ways to express the unity of all creation.

And so it is that when you find the beautiful and exotic star fruit, known, grown and enjoyed since ancient times, and you slice it in a cross-sectional format to eat, you find the ultimate expression of this star symbol of creation that will unfold in your mouth to provide you with the nourishment of antioxidants and nutrients that provide your star-originated spirit the catalysts for growing new stars within. And by this we mean the atoms within your bodies, which are themselves structured like stars, with small nuclei, surrounded by a pattern and dusting of electrons, not orbiting just in the manner of a solar system, but moving here and there in a quantum phenomena, almost spiraling and dancing in spiritual ecstasy.

And, indeed, all of nature, all of creation is steeped with the symbology of the pentagram, the 5-pointed-star and the golden ratio, propagating growth along the lines of the golden divine proportion of the archetypes of universal divine creation. Whether you look at the phi ratio in the Fibonacci sequence of spiraling leaves around a central stem in a plant, or what we call phyllotaxis, or at the phi ratios involved in the stepping down of electromagnetic energies from solar systems to stars to planets in a spiracular dissemination of the breath of God, you will understand that the golden proportion of being is the breath of live that informs all of creation.

And so it is that the star fruit, a visual and literal and tasty representation of the star pentagram structure, in its cross-section, reveals to us not only the fact of how the phi ratio can create a symmetrical geometry that makes us feel happy and reminds us that we are stars (in that, as we have mentioned before that all the lines of this star cross in phi ratios), but also the fact that the 5 points themselves and the replication of 5 in our human bodies, with 5 fingers on each hand, five toes on each feet, remind us of the complexity and synastry of the 5th element, that quintessence of Spirit, that animates and enfolds all of creation, breathing the breath of life into the four elements of air, water, earth and fire, animating your physical bodies with the essence of Spirit, activating and anchoring in your Spirit into a human body, generating life in a format that is beamed down in spiracular form, along the lines of the phi ratios, through sun systems into your human body, thus activating the cells and atoms within to vibrate themselves like stars, creating the fruits of life within the body of your everyday reality, and hence creating star fruits in the form of human beings who are actually stars expressing their manifested pentagrammatic phi ratios as 3rd dimensional organisms walking and talking in earthly manifestation.

Now, as the Earth ascends to its higher vibration of being, now that the Shift in consciousness moves your planet to the next swirl of its own path of growth, on its own axis of phyllotaxis growth, you are being provided an opportunity to excite your atoms, your cells, your very DNA and RNA to higher frequential vibrations, to higher expressions of their star nature.

You could also think of this opportunity as getting a gold star now instead of a blue or red or green one. For all the basic colors of your Earthly existence are about to take on an added resonant hue, glinting with the freshness of a higher vibrational resonance, the knowledge of a deeper connection to Source, and of an intrinsic and intuitive understanding of your star self, and so your inner star vibrates in harmony to the phi ratios of being, and so your intrinsic star nature is validated in multidimensional forms, echoing in chambers of reverberation all across the heavens.

And so as you eat your star fruit and you contemplate your intrinsic star nature, know that you are about to become, with the ongoing Shift in consciousness, more fully conscious of the geometry of the golden ratios that establish your connection to Source. You are about to claim your inner Star, which has always been present, but which was often hidden amongst your many lifetimes, under cloaks of feeling small, being told that you are worth nothing, that you need validation from others, that you need to conform to others' rules to get the external star of validation.

And as you do this, you will begin to vibrate at a golden frequency of understanding and you will spread out your hands and feet and feel the 5-fold symmetry within your toes, your fingers, the very cells of your body that embody the Fibonnaci sequence of alignment, whether in the ratio of your finger to your arm or other proportions of your body, expressing the golden ratio of being in a very conscious way.[46] And you will feel fantastic. You will feel on top of the world. You will be your own golden star, your own beautiful star fruit, awarding the star to yourself by just acknowledging consciously the star being within.

And as you claim your star-heritage and divine wisdom you will begin to leave behind the reaction and judgement to any situation that comes your way in life. You will begin to observe with a detached, higher perspective, a golden perspective of insight, which acknowledges that all of creation, whether a positive experience or a negative experience from a 3rd dimensional perspective, is derived from a common thread of creation that starts from the infinity of the Supreme Being and spirals down to your everyday reality in a way that is perfect; for every experience is one to be cherished as an opportunity for soul growth around the spiral of phyllotaxic growth as you move to higher octaves of your own vibration.

And you will find your star-divine neutrality will aid your compassion for yourself and for all of humanity. You will understand that every other being is a star being as well. And with your neutrality to combative and aggressive frequencies of anger, hate, fear, and dissolution, you will offer divine compassion, allowing the potentials for neutralizing these frequencies which belonged to a lower octave of creation, and now no longer will be able to procreate at the higher level of gold-star vibration that all of humanity and Gaia is moving to. And so, you, as a star being, will be helping awaken to conscious star-awareness your human family that is around you, as they discover the star fruit within themselves.

Papaya—*Pentagons Create Dodecahedral Geometries that allow for Higher Vibrational Realities of Orange-Gold Creativity and Connectivity*

Whenever there is a desire to satisfy the deepest urges within us, whenever there is a desire to ripen into the open that which has been suppressed and subdued, that is a good indication of deep healing that is taking place, of the ascension of our own selves into higher vibrational realities where we accept all that we are, all that we have been, and all the potentials of what we can be.

And so it is, that we wish to discuss the papaya fruit today, as a symbol, not only of the tropical ripe expressions of our celebration of our complete selves, reveling in the orange, fleshy hues of succulent taste and juiciness, but also as a symbol of the inherent geometric self-similarity that defines the fractal nature of Nature and unites all of creation from the emblematic patterns of fruits of ripe expression to the anchoring of the planetary grids of ascension.

When you split open a papaya you are enriched by the sights, sounds and smells of ripe, fleshy orange fruit that is full of the enzymes and antioxidants that nurture your body, cleansing it of impurities, giving it the space to release that which no longer serves it as it is now able to move to higher vibrational aspects of itself, aligned with health, wealth and the lack of disease.

And to reach this flesh, you release and remove all those pearl-like black caviar dots of seedlings within that hearken to the dark underside of your experiences that are at the core of what you have gone through in the world of duality that is now ending, and that you symbolically release and remove to access the fleshy, higher-vibrational, orange, almost golden vibrations of yourself.

And you will notice as you slice your papaya that if you cut it open lengthwise, you will be faced, in the cross-section with the eye of duality peering back at you, filled with these black pearls of dualistic experience that you have picked up along the way.

The eye, which represents all of your experiences is to be embraced and alighted anew as you remove the black seeds, turning what was a mixed color spectrum of black and orange to one that is orange alone, transforming the eye into an eye of Horus that can help you connect to more multidimensional aspects of yourself that live in the higher octaves of all of reality.

And with this new orange eye of Horus, you allow yourself the possibility to see it all, to see the self-similarity of the fractal nature of Nature, as you absorb and process the divine process of creation in its simplicity and its beauty, crowned with the orange glow of creativity that you absorb within, as you bite into the fleshy, orange, vibration-increasing papaya flesh that awaits your awakening.

For you notice now that if you were to slice the papaya in a cross-wise cross-section, the plane of the cut will reveal a pentagon shape inside, filled with the black pearls of past dualistic experience. And this pentagon shape enfolds within its outline the 5-pointed star that we have described before, in our discussion of the star fruit, and that is in itself a combination of phi angles and phi ratios, for the golden ratio that is the limit of the Fibonacci sequence, is indeed the basis for fractal creation at the very smallest levels of creation to the largest, as all proceeds in a self-replicating manner.

Even within this pentagon of the papaya's cross-section, as you remove the black seeds of the past and heighten the orange creative glow of the future, you will notice the existence of nascent triangles within the pentagon that are circumscribed as golden triangles, the ratios of the sides expressing this self-same phi ratio of 1.61803. And you realize that within each symmetry of creation, lies a greater mystery and unfolding, that which is often beyond what meets the eye, that which is often beyond the comprehension of dualistic logic-trained analysis, and closer to the understanding of the simplicity of all of creation that follows the same pattern.

And we would encourage all of you budding scientists and young ones here who are looking for that quantum insight for new discoveries and contributions to humanity's ascension to look at the ancient principle of Occam's razor as a substitute for pure logical analysis. For it is within the simplicity of design, in seeing the grander heuristic of the overall pattern that you begin to understand all of creation, returning once again to the higher vibrational knowledge that is the hallmark of the Creator-God that you are inside, vibrating with the orange-gold flavors and vibrations of higher knowledge and divinity.

And so, with the insight of a higher vibrational Creator God, you abstract out the pentagon shape from within the cross section of this orange papaya, and you, in your mind's eye, see it combining with eleven other cross-sectional pentagon shapes, with all 12 coming together to form a dodecahedron, that Platonic solid of 12 sides and beautiful convex symmetry that conveys the beauty of geometric alignment and connection. It also, in its numerology, conveys the notion of the 12 dimensions of the Milky Way galaxy coming together to form the whole of the connection that is being collectively raised to a higher vibrational unit as the Shift in consciousness proceeds, affecting not only your planet, but the wider cosmos, as the photon rays of the higher dispensations of golden-orange liquid light and love vibrations spread across this region of all there is.

The dodecahedron has been understood and acknowledged as a beautiful platonic solid that is found replicated in nature not only in that the faces of its pentagon building blocks are found in the cross-sections of fruits like the papaya and the star fruit, but also in the very construction and realization of the phi ratios that are the implicit parameters that allow for the overall dodecahedron to be assembled, as these ratios derive from the Fibonnaci sequence which drive the helical, spiracular aspects of most growth in the Universe, as seen in our descriptions of flower and fruits, but certainly not limited to these, for you can extend the principles also to the birth of stars, galaxies and universes, .

And it is now, as the Shift in consciousness moves to its final phases that we wish all of humanity to realize that this is not only about saying the time has come for a change, but 2012 counts, or the process of moving towards 2012 counts because of the geometric alignment of a new crystalline grid that has been anchored across the circumference of the Earth, and as it comes more fully into place as the limit to the winter solstice in 2012 is approached, more and more changes will become an everyday reality.

And so it is that we wish to point out that this new crystalline grid of ascension is composed of 12 faces that interlock together in what is, at its core, a dodecahedral structure. But what is interesting, in terms of the fractal nature of Nature, and how self-replication and division allows for new vibrations of geometry to create new higher dimensional realities and consciousnesses, is that these 12 faces can be stellated with each face giving rise to a 5-sided pyramid, which each side representing an isosceles triangle of golden divination. And with the fractal nature of Nature, we can further sub-divide each triangle into two, creating a double-stellated dodecahedron, one where each pentagonal face has not only its own base plus 5 triangles as facets, for a total of six facets per face, but, then, the self-similar process of division that is fractal allows for a division into the double-penta format allowing for 12 facets per face, leading to the 144 facets that create this new dodecahedral geometry of ascension for your planet that follows the same principles of phi ratios and pentagonal symmetry that are found in fruits and flowers and the growth patterns of all there is.

And so it is that we encourage you, as you bite into delicious fruits like the orange-golden papaya, as you grow in the orange-based higher vibrational insights that come from clearing out the occlusions of duality that obscured with logical mish-mash your internal eye of Horus's clear understanding of the Occam's razor simplicity in principle that underlies all the complexity and wonder of Nature that is at the heart of all there is, to acknowledge and appreciate that you are a Creator-God and you are beginning to understand that you already know how everything works, that everything is connected, and all the information lies within the eye of Horus, that is your 3rd eye to be reclaimed and understood.

And as you, in your higher vibrational state, growing with the fruits of knowledge and intuitive understanding, claim this higher quantum self, you will understand the fruits of this ascension process as it allows you to merge with higher multidimensional aspects of self, that are able to see it all, absorb it all, and create anew with the fractal building blocks that are simple yet create the wonderful creations in all Universes, with the ingenuity of a higher wisdom of innate geometry that underlies all of creation.

Know that your ascension is assured if you so choose to seek it. Know that as you begin to embrace how all of humanity, how all of creation is united, how all of Spirit is spiritually aligned geometrically with the golden connections of spiracular creation and golden ratios, you will be raising your frequency forever, as you move from linear time and a 3rd dimensional and dualistic reality, to one of simultaneous time, a 4th or 5th dimensional or higher reality and one that is fully cognizant of one vibration of golden-orange connection, fitting in the phi ratios into geometric building blocks like the pentagon, creating new geometries of growth and ascension, like the 144-faceted crystalline grid.

Jackfruit—*Opening Your Reality Via Axiotonal Lines of Ever-present Connection*

Although the jackfruit is not readily available in the Western world, it is becoming increasingly well-known in those specialty markets that sell healthy products. For it is beginning to be recognized for the ancient wisdom and truth it contains in its deceptively plain-toned colors of flesh inside a brownish, unadorned casing.

It is a fruit that delivers its nourishment and sustenance in a multi-varied way, for it both calms the spirit as well as provides nutrients for your body. It is a wise, sage-like fruit that knows that your body's essence needs support and succor far beyond the apparent and immediate physical needs.

And so it is that the jackfruit, in its small, many-coned exterior, suggests a conical expansion of all there is, inviting you to break open this shell of many pine-cones, perhaps intimating that beneath the dull, plain and understated exterior is a new undulating reality, one that can, through the conings of absolution and dissolution of your bodily self, connect you with aspects of your multi-dimensional self, for you are Atmanic, you are everything and everyone, as you ascend in consciousness.

And as you use the conings of protrusions on the exterior of the jackfruit you find yourself unveiling an interior full of the complexities of your own beingness and connectedness as a sovereign being and as a being connected to much more: higher aspects of yourself and others as well, for in the higher aspects of yourself, you and others are the same.

As you smell the jackfruit's odor, the pungency indicates a return to sensation, a return to vibrancy, an enhancement and an attunement of the bodily senses to a higher vibration of allowing, knowledge and wisdom. The odor wraps a mist of undulating caresses around your etheric bodies as you now pare open pieces of flesh that are encased within the pockets of harder casings. The flesh radiates out in spokes from the central core of this jackfruit. It is fleshy, creamy and delicious, in this internal, now-exposed form. It is primordial desire and joy, waiting to be molded and enjoyed as you consume the higher experience of yourself and allow the fires of creativity within to be ignited.

It yields it creamy self to you, as spokes of your multidimensional raw, fiery self now connect you to a central core of group consciousness, just as the fresh, yielding fruit itself is connected to the core pith from whence it grows. And as this connection is acknowledged and celebrated anew, you find a spinning of yourself into a starbeing coming into fruition. For in reality you are a being from the stars, a multidimensional being that incarnated on Earth many times in anticipation of this imminent return home to the heart of God.

And the central core of the jackfruit connects your many selves back to itself, just as you find and rediscover the axiotonal lines that are beginning to anchor into your etheric bodies as the Shift in consciousness proceeds, and you find those connections that appeared to be severed under the illusion of separation under the Earth game, but which are actually ever-present, ever-loving, ever-expanding.[47]

Imagine yourself now as a piece of flesh within this jackfruit. Yes, you placed yourself within a human body, just as the flesh is kept within a casing. Yes, you shrouded yourself with a hard exterior, as in the exterior of this fruit. Yes, you still somehow knew that there was divinity within you, which is why, like the cones on the exterior of the jackfruit suggesting a geometric connection to Source, you, too, expressed divinity in many ways through the creations of your Earthly experiences, whether in music, dance, theatre, cinema, writing, speaking, loving, nurturing or simply being creative at home or in your job.

And now the Shift in consciousness is bringing your awareness back to the central core of your fundamental truth and reality; and, as it does this, you are beginning to acknowledge the many other pieces of flesh that are yourself that have played this game in other incarnations. By this we mean not only the other incarnations you have had, but the incarnations that other souls have had as well, for they all go into the Akashic records recording the annals of history within the 3rd dimensional experiment of free will called Earth.

And as this recollection and understanding seeps into the very core of your being, you find yourself yanked to a higher perspective of group consciousness via the axiotonal lines of growing and ever-present connection that reveal to you that you are all, you have always been all, for it is from Unity that you originally sprang to play this game of duality, among other games of manifested Universes, galaxies and planets along the way.

And yes, you are now waking up to higher levels of understanding. And yes, you are beginning to feel true love and compassion for yourself and for others, for your community, and even for others of different skin colors, religions and origins that you have never met for indeed you might have been one of these yourself at some point in this Earthly experiment.

And so, like a jack of all trades, you, this fleshy part of you now acknowledges the jackfruit of experience that has always been about staying connected and remembering this connection to Source and to all, even though the veils of illusion of your 3rd dimensional reality provided a convenient amnesia for a while, allowing you to create those human experiences that you will cherish and rejoice in; yes, even the difficult experiences, my dear ones, for these experiences allowed you to grow as a soul, back to the understandings of group consciousness that are now dawning in your reality.

For the unpleasant experiences, once creating karma via the **Law of Fair Exchange**, in this game of free will on Earth, now, as the Shift in consciousness proceeds apace, allow you to wake up. Each shock gives you an opportunity to tether a new awareness of an already existing axiotonal line back to Source, for you have been it all, you have done it all, as you reclaim the Jack that you are, as you find the larger jackfruit body your flesh is encased and supported in.

And it is through the support and love and divine light of the central core of your jackfruit experiences that holds the fruit together, that allows it to emanate its smells of the vibrations of this 3rd dimensional experience. This is the gift, the vibration of all experiences that you take with you, recorded in the Akashic records, as you now begin the journey home.

Welcome to the dawning of a new age of collective consciousness while still a piece of connected flesh, via axiotonal lines, on an ascending Earth plane.

Golden-Orange Tomato—*Finding and Expressing Divinity Within, Across Simultaneous Time*

By the end of any undertaking, at that moment of imminent conclusion, there is often a sense of doubt, a question within as to whether the conclusion is indeed complete, whether you have imbibed all that you need from the nectars of knowledge that have been revealed to you as part of your learning and awakening.

And this doubt is released not by knowing that the undertaking, or, in this case, that this book, has captured all that you need to grow or awaken. It is not in knowing that this is the bible of all that you will ever need to read, sound, taste or smell within the images of fruits, flowers, birds and colors inspired within you.

But, it is in fact released and transformed into gratitude and excitement in the knowledge that this is only the beginning of a very personal journey of growth, transformation and awakening for you, as you transform yourself from the earthly, earth-bound human you have always recognized yourself as, to a 4th and 5th dimensional being that is fully awakened and understands the potentials that lie ahead for future growth.

For it is in understanding that this undertaking, this book has planted the seeds for your transformation into an heirloom variety of growth, one that takes you from the basic fruit of divine knowledge housed within a human vessel, to a particular golden orange heirloom variety of yourself, one that is unique in its flavours and divinations of all, that you embrace the vinous, spiracular, miraculous and amazing growth into your Higher Selves, as the Shift in consciousness proceeds apace.

And as this takes place, you, with your own particular vibration of higher heirloom color and shape, will find that you are much larger than you ever expected. You will find, in your spiracular growth, that reflects the nature of Nature, that you are connected with golden ratios and golden connections in the phyllotaxis of your growth by Fibonnacci sequences, to other aspects of yourself.

In fact, you begin to realize that group consciousness is indeed higher consciousness, and that the higher you grow and reach, you find your heirloom variety of self connecting with and combining with others who you thought were separate in a limited and veiled 3rd dimensional reality, which is now rapidly ending.

And so with any ending, there is always a new beginning. And, indeed, as this book comes to a close, we encourage you to seek out the opportunities and vistas that reflect your passions deep inside, those vibrations of creativity that make your heart sing like the song of a beautiful bird, celebrating the blooming of the flowers of your ascension, in the ranges of shapes and colors and hues that make up your very own unique, harmonious and divine self.

For, like any heirloom tomato that is deservedly prized, you are juicy and fertile inside. Your taste is delicious, for it has been carefully cultivated and allowed to flourish over eons of time.

And these eons of time that we refer to end up ultimately, in this new beginning of consciousness, to be simultaneous time, as your realize, in your golden orange vibrations of higher connections, that you have always been large, vast, grand, glorious and uniquely you.

And it is these very unique heirloom gifts, colors, vibrations and shapes that define the geometry of your eternal divine being that you have come to share with humanity and the world that is now ascending rapidly into higher consciousness, at this most momentous time of change.

So we encourage you, dear one, to step forward with alacrity onto your path of self-discovery. Discover the geometry of self-similarity to all of the golden ratios of nature that define Nature, including your nature.

And in your divine vibrations of self, connect with the divine natures of others, and find the vibrations that best establish a harmonious and divine connection. Move to the vibrations of love and light, creating golden rectangles, golden triangles and golden means in your dealings and unveilings of self with others.

And so you find an effervescent self emerging, full of the joy of simply being, full of the anticipation of the excitement of your journey, as you use this book as a platform to grow further, to explore further and manifest your highest divine blueprint of heirloom and golden orange destiny that you came here to express and to share.

Your light shines bright now as you become more and more golden with the golden light of the divine essence of yourself, sharing the orange creativity that is the hallmark of divinity as you travel down the road of your divine destiny now with a new vibration of understanding of where you are heading.

We, on behalf of all the authors and contributors to this journey with you so far, salute your intrepidity in joining humanity at this time, for being part of this grand project of ascension, and for contributing your heirloom variety of self to the world to share.

We promise you that you will be much cherished by both yourselves and by others as you continue to grow into the divine being that you already are.

And so, within the halls of simultaneous time, for every ending there is a beginning, for there is really no ending and no beginning, it is simply experience, and you choose and create every experience as you grow higher and more beautiful in the vibration of golden orange heirloom light.

Many blessings, and may roses and flowers and rainbow colors be strewn your way always as you take flight and display the fruits of your heirloom self in the blossoming of your conscious awareness.

Appendix 1
Chakra Healing Index

The 99 Pieces and Chakras Healed

#1 **Maple Tree** -*Rooting Yourself to Inner Joy*   Root, Heart & Crown

#2 **Gold**- *Know Your Intrinsic Value*   Solar Plexus

#3 **Green**—*The Emerald Light of Unity*   Heart

#4 **Pink**—*An Airy Sweetness of Awareness*   Sacral & Crown

#5 **Yellow**—*The Beam Leading You To Your Destiny*   Solar Plexus

#6 **Caramel** -*Bringing Out the Sweetness in Yourself*   Throat

#7 **Orange**—*The Glowing Igniter of Your Divine Self*   Root & Sacral

#8 **Blue**—*A Regal Expression of the Authentic Self*   Root & Throat

#9 **Purple**—*Astounding Awareness*   Throat & Crown

#10 **Red**—*Grounding and Expressing the Will of the Creator*   Root & Crown

#11 **Turquoise**—*Believe That You Are Magic*   Solar Plexus & 3rd Eye

#12 **Navy Blue**—*The Ocean Warrior*   Solar Plexus & Heart

#13 **Mauve**—*Baptize Your Inner Angel*   Heart & Crown

#14 **Parrot**—*Messenger, Not Mimicer*   Root, Sacral, Heart, Crown

#15 **Canary**—*Yellow Harbinger to Your Destiny*   Root, Solar Plexus, 3rd Eye

#16 **Cuckoo**—*A Dance to Inner Time*   Sacral, Solar Plexus

#17 **Finch**—*Into the Urban Woods We Go, Expessing Our Superlativeness*   Heart & Crown

#18 **Robin**—*Expressing and Experiencing Life With Abandon*   Root, Solar Plexus, Crown

#19 **Bluebird**—*Noting the Blue Certainty and Taking Flight Today*   Root, Solar Plexus, Heart

#20 **Cherry Tree**—*Red Fruit and Blossoming Flowers On Display in Your 2nd Chakra*   Sacral & Heart

#21 **Blueberry**—*A Naughty Psychic Adventure*   Sacral, Throat, 3rd Eye

#22 **Banana**—*A Stable, Harmonious Symphony of Growth*   Root, Sacral, Solar Plexus

#23 **Apple**—*A Dear Gift of Balance*   Sacral & Solar Plexus

#24 **Plum**—*Union of Spirit and Matter*   Root, Solar Plexus, Crown

#25 **Cherry**—*A Saucy, Vivacious Tumble*   Sacral, Solar Plexus, Heart

#26 **Watermelon**—*The Creator Within* Heart & Crown

#27 **Cranberry**—*Taste Your Dreams* Solar Plexus & Throat

#28 **Date**—*Sweet Sustenance For Your Inner Child* Sacral & Heart

#29 **Grapefruit**—*Complexity for the Soul* Sacral, Solar Plexus, Heart

#30 **Guava**—*Milk of Life* Solar Plexus, Heart, Crown

#31 **Mango**—*Remember Your God-Self* Root, Solar Plexus, Crown

#32 **Orange**—*Willfulness Abated* Root, Sacral, Solar Plexus

#33 **Oak Tree**—*Embodying the 3ʳᵈ Chakra* Sacral, Solar Plexus

#34 **Olive Green**—*Ontological Joie de Vivre* Root, Sacral, Solar Plexus

#35 **Brown**—*Murky Happenstance Overcome* Root, Sacral, Solar Plexus, Heart

#36 **Emerald Green**—*Gleaming, Gloaming Through Life* Sacral, Solar Plexus, Heart, 3ʳᵈ Eye , Crown

#37 **Magenta**—*Conductor of Your Magical Soul* Sacral, Solar Plexus, 3ʳᵈ Eye, Crown

#38 **Aquamarine**—*Folding Into Your Divine Self* Heart, 3ʳᵈ Eye, Crown

#39 **Rust Orange**—*Galvanized Beacons of Light* Sacral, Solar Plexus, Heart

#40 **Cobalt Blue**—*Mine Your Life Into a Beauteous Expression of Your Destiny* Root, Sacral, Solar Plexus

#41 **Tan**—*From Fossil to Cosmic Being* Root, Solar Plexus, Crown

#42 **Indigo**—*Return to the Source of Certainty and Co-Creation* Root, Solar Plexus, Heart, Crown

#43 **Lime Green**—*Astringent Cleanser of Wounding* — Sacral, Solar Plexus

#44 **Fuchsia**—*Remembering the Particles of Higher Intelligence* — Solar Plexus, 3rd Eye, Crown

#45 **Lemon-Lime**—*Express Your Fizzy, Effervescent Self with Confidence* — Root, Solar Plexus, Heart, Throat

#46 **Willow Tree**—*Weeping and Loving All So Deeply* — Heart, Throat

#47 **Rose**—*Primal "Rosa" Red of Source* — Heart, Crown

#48 **Primrose**—*Pale Harbinger of Spiritual Awakening* — Root, Heart, Crown

#49 **Foxglove**—*Fitting into the Shroud* — Root, Heart, Crown

#50 **Hibiscus**—*Kneel to Your Inner Soul* — Root, Sacral, Solar Plexus, Heart, Crown

#51 **Rhododendron**—*Portal to Multidimensionality* — Sacral, Solar Plexus, Heart

#52 **Sunflower**—*A Shower of Limitless Light* — Root, Sacral, Heart, Crown

#53 **Poppy**—*Billow Into Your Dreams* — Heart, 3rd Eye

#54 **Daffodil**—*Golden, Honeyed Host* — Sacral, Heart, Crown

#55 **Heliotrope**—*Unmasking, Transforming the Demon Within* — Root, Sacral, Solar Plexus, Heart

#56 **Forsythia**—*Golden Bells Are Ringing* — Root, Solar Plexus, Heart, Crown

#57 **Forget-Me-Not**—*Tantric Communion* — Sacral, Heart

#58 **Hyacinth**—*Lucky Pattern of Individual Unity* — Root, Solar Plexus, Heart, Crown

#59 **Hydrangea**—*From Scrooge to Blooming Community* — Root, Solar Plexus, Heart, Crown

#60 **Poppy—Part 2—***Alchemical Transformation of the Self Through Love* — Root, Sacral, Solar Plexus, Heart

#61 **Beech Tree**—*Logos of Life in Your Throat Chakra* — Sacral, Solar Plexus, Heart, Throat, Crown

#62 **Parakeet**—*Familiarity Absconds Reality* — Solar Plexus, Throat, Crown

#63 **Sparrow**—*Divine Providence Delivered* — Root, Sacral, Solar Plexus, Heart, Throat

#64 **Starling**—*Resist Not A Call To Your Star Family* — Root, Heart, Throat, Crown

#65 **Magpie** *Reveling, Revealing a Maverick Within* — Sacral, Solar Plexus, Heart, Throat

#66 **Swan**—*Golden Rebirthing* — Root, Sacral, Heart, Crown

#67 **Peacock**—*Uncloak Your 100 Eyes* — Solar Plexus, Throat, 3rd Eye

#68 **Lemon**—*Nostalgia Creates Anew* — Sacral, Solar Plexus, Throat, 3rd Eye, Crown

#69 **Blackberry** *Re-vision Your Communication* — Solar Plexus, Throat, Crown

#70 **Raspberry**—*Indicate Who You Are, Facilitate Your Survival* — Sacral, Solar Plexus, Throat, Crown

#71 **Tomato**—*Bursting Forth Into Group Consciousness* — Root, Heart, Crown

#72 **Pear**—*Milky, Nurturing Fruit of the Creator* — Root, Sacral, Solar Plexus, Crown

#73 **Pineapple**- *Honey and Manna from Reconstitution* — Root, Sacral, Throat, 3rd Eye

#74 **Pine Tree**—*Transgressing and Weaving a New Reality With Your 3rd Eye*   Root, 3rd Eye, Crown

#75 **Vermilion**—*Ordinary Twilight witching Summons a Higher Self*   Root, 3rd Eye, Crown

#76 **Lilac**—*A Lighter Path to Honeyed, Cinnamoned Acceptance of Sanctity*   Sacral, Solar Plexus, Crown

#77 **Platinum**—*Join the Inclusive Angelic Choir*   Root, Sacral, Solar Plexus, 3rd Eye, Crown

#78 **White**—*Representations of Reality Revealed*   Root, Solar Plexus, Throat, Crown

#79 **Burnt Ochre**—*Salaam to the Glowing Eternal Being That You Are*   Root, Sacral, Crown

#80 **Wisteria**—*Pruning a Vine, Blooming Forever*   Root, Sacral, Solar Plexus, Heart, Crown

#81 **Crimson**—*Artifice, Shed Before, Becomes a Mantle of Higher Glory*   Root, Sacral, Solar Plexus, Heart, Crown

#82 **Mango**—*Ripening the Sun-God Within*   Root, Solar Plexus, Crown

#83 **Parrot Green**—*Mimicking and Spreading Joy, Healing Others Along the Way*   Solar Plexus, Heart, Throat

#84 **Taupe**—*Ordinary to Extraordinary and Celestial*   Sacral, Solar Plexus, Heart

#85 **Red Rose**—*Creating a Rose Garden of Love on Earth*   Root, Sacral, Heart, Crown

#86 **Silver**—*Bursting Into the New You*   Heart, 3rd Eye, Crown

#87 **Ash Tree**—*Rekindling the Inner Crown*   Crown

#88 **Lily**—*Heartfelt Purity*   Sacral, Solar Plexus, Heart, Crown

#89 **Water Lily**—*Rebirthing the Sun-God Within*   Root, Solar Plexus, Crown

#90 **Dandelion**—*Parachuting into a New Beginning*   Root, Heart, 3rd Eye, Crown

#91 **Squash Blossoms**—*Star Blossoming Into Ascension*   Root, Sacral, Heart, Crown

#92 **Shamrock**—*Understanding the Trinity Within*   Solar Plexus, Heart, Crown

#93 **Sunflower**—*Unfolding Geometrically Into Your Glorious Golden Potential*   Root, Heart, Crown

#94 **Ananas**—*Sprightly Ascension into the Helical Construction of the Fiery Red Group Alignments of Higher Vibrational Reality*   Root, Heart, Crown

#95 **Pomegranate**—*Trinitizing the Self into Spherical Unity*   Root, Sacral, Solar Plexus, Heart, Crown

#96 **Star Fruit**—*Revering the Self as the Divine Image of Infinity*   Root, Solar Plexus, Heart, Crown

#97 **Papaya**—*Pentagons Create Dodecahedral Geometries that allow for Higher Vibrational Realities of Orange-Gold Creativity and Connectivity*   Solar Plexus, 3rd Eye, Crown

#98 **Jackfruit**—*Opening Your Reality
Via Axiotonal Lines of Ever-present
Connection*   All Chakras

#99 **Golden- Orange Tomato**—*Finding
and Expressing Divinity Within,
Across Simultaneous Time*   All Chakras

Appendix 2
Sprit Collaborators Index

The 99 Pieces and Spirit Collaborators

#1 **Maple Tree** -*Rooting Yourself to Inner Joy* — Archangel Gabriel & Mother Mary

#2 **Gold**- *Know Your Intrinsic Value* — Hathors

#3 **Green**—*The Emerald Light of Unity* — Ra

#4 **Pink**—*An Airy Sweetness of Awareness* — Hathors

#5 **Yellow**—*The Beam Leading You To Your Destiny* — Archangel Michael

#6 **Caramel** -*Bringing Out the Sweetness in Yourself* — Mother Mary

#7 **Orange**—*The Glowing Igniter of Your Divine Self* — Kuthumi

#8 **Blue**—*A Regal Expression of the Authentic Self* — Hathors

#9 **Purple**—*Astounding Awareness* — Hathors

#10 **Red**—*Grounding and Expressing the Will of the Creator* — Hathors

#11 **Turquoise**—*Believe That You Are Magic* — Kuthumi

#12 **Navy Blue**—*The Ocean Warrior*   Kuthumi & Lao-Tzu

#13 **Mauve**—*Baptize Your Inner Angel*   Lao-Tzu

#14 **Parrot**—*Messenger, Not Mimicer*   Genoa

#15 **Canary**—*Yellow Harbinger to Your Destiny*   Ismael & Jacob

#16 **Cuckoo**—*A Dance to Inner Time*   Jan & Hiawatha

#17 **Finch**—*Into the Urban Woods We Go, Expessing Our Superlativeness*   Goddess Hathor & Hiawatha

#18 **Robin**—*Expressing and Experiencing Life With Abandon*   Charles Dickens & Hiawatha

#19 **Bluebird**—*Noting the Blue Certainty and Taking Flight Today*   Hathors & Charles Dickens

#20 **Cherry Tree**—*Red Fruit and Blossoming Flowers On Display in Your 2nd Chakra*   Hathors, Ra & Mother Mary

#21 **Blueberry**—*A Naughty Psychic Adventure*   Mother Mary

#22 **Banana**—*A Stable, Harmonious Symphony of Growth*   Kuthumi

#23 **Apple**—*A Dear Gift of Balance* Kuthumi

#24 **Plum**—*Union of Spirit and Matter*   Kuthumi & Mother Mary

#25 **Cherry**—*A Saucy, Vivacious Tumble*   Kuthumi

#26 **Watermelon**—*The Creator Within*   Kuthumi & Mother Mary

#27 **Cranberry**—*Taste Your
Dreams*   Kuthumi

#28 **Date**—*Sweet Sustenance For
Your Inner Child*   Kuthumi

#29 **Grapefruit**—*Complexity
for the Soul*   Mother Mary

#30 **Guava**—*Milk of Life*   Kuthumi & Mother Mary

#31 **Mango**—*Remember
Your God-Self*   Kuthumi

#32 **Orange**—*Willfulness
Abated*   Hathors

#33 **Oak Tree**—*Embodying
the 3rd Chakra*   Hathors & Archangel Rafael

#34 **Olive Green**—*Ontological
Joie de Vivre*   Ismael & Kahlil Gibran

#35 **Brown**—*Murky
Happenstance Overcome*   Hathors & Archangel
Gabriel

#36 **Emerald Green**—*Gleaming,
Gloaming Through Life*   Hathors & Charles Dickens

#37 **Magenta**—*Conductor of
Your Magical Soul*   Mother Mary

#38 **Aquamarine**—*Folding Into
Your Divine Self*   Hathors & Kahlil Gibran

#39 **Rust Orange**—*Galvanized
Beacons of Light*   Hathors & Hiawatha

#40 **Cobalt Blue**—*Mine Your
Life Into a Beauteous
Expression of Your Destiny*   Ismael

#41 **Tan**—*From Fossil to
Cosmic Being*   Hathors & Charles Dickens

#42 **Indigo**—*Return to the
Source of Certainty and
Co-Creation*   Hathors & Hiawatha

#43 **Lime Green**—*Astringent Cleanser of Wounding* — Hiawatha & Hathors

#44 **Fuchsia**—*Remembering the Particles of Higher Intelligence* — Hiawatha & Charles Dickens

#45 **Lemon-Lime**—*Express Your Fizzy, Effervescent Self with Confidence* — Goddess Hathor & Hiawatha

#46 **Willow Tree**—*Weeping and Loving All So Deeply* — Hathors, Mary Magdalene & Ra

#47 **Rose**—*Primal "Rosa" Red of Source* — Kuthumi

#48 **Primrose**—*Pale Harbinger of Spiritual Awakening* — Kuthumi

#49 **Foxglove**—*Fitting into the Shroud* — Archangel Rafael & Hathors

#50 **Hibiscus**—*Kneel to Your Inner Soul* — Hathors & Kampala

#51 **Rhododendron**—*Portal to Multidimensionality* — Lao-Tzu

#52 **Sunflower**—*A Shower of Limitless Light* — Lao-Tzu & Hathors

#53 **Poppy**—*Billow Into Your Dreams* — Kahlil Gibran

#54 **Daffodil**—*Golden, Honeyed Host* — Hathors & Najimi

#55 **Heliotrope**—*Unmasking, Transforming the Demon Within* — Kahlil Gibran & Hathors

#56 **Forsythia**—*Golden Bells Are Ringing* — Hiawatha & Hathors

#57 **Forget-Me-Not**—*Tantric Communion* — Kahlil Gibran & Hathors

#74 **Pine Tree**—*Transgressing and Weaving a New Reality With Your 3rd Eye* — Archangel Gabriel & Mother Mary

#75 **Vermilion**—*Ordinary Twilight Bewitching Summons a Higher Self* — Lord Buddha & Mother Mary

#76 **Lilac**—*A Lighter Path to Honeyed, Cinnamoned Acceptance of Sanctity* — Lao-Tzu & Hathors

#77 **Platinum**—*Join the Inclusive Angelic Choir* — Hathors & Hiawatha

#78 **White**—*Representations of Reality Revealed* — Hiawatha & Lady Guinevere

#79 **Burnt Ochre**—*Salaam to the Glowing Eternal Being That You Are* — Shakespeare & Hiawatha

#80 **Wisteria**—*Pruning a Vine, Blooming Forever* — Lao-Tzu & Hathors

#81 **Crimson**—*Artifice, Shed Before, Becomes a Mantle of Higher Glory* — Hiawatha & Archangel Gabriel

#82 **Mango**—*Ripening the Sun-God Within* — Lao-Tzu & Hathors

#83 **Parrot Green**—*Mimicking and Spreading Joy, Healing Others Along the Way* — Hathors & Charles Dickens

#84 **Taupe**—*Ordinary to Extraordinary and Celestial* — Mother Mary & Hiawatha

#85 **Red Rose**—*Creating a Rose Garden of Love on Earth* — Robert Burns & Hiawatha

#86 **Silver**—*Bursting Into the New You* — Merlin & Hathors

#87 **Ash Tree**—*Rekindling the Inner Crown* — Archangel Gabriel & Mother Mary

#88 **Lily**—*Heartfelt Purity* Kuthumi & Hathors

#89 **Water Lily**—*Rebirthing the* Kuthumi & Archangel
Sun-God Within Michael

#90 **Dandelion**—*Parachuting*
into a New Beginning Jerome & Kuthumi

#91 **Squash Blossoms**—*Star*
Blossoming Into Ascension Kuthumi & Jerome

#92 **Shamrock**—*Understanding*
the Trinity Within Kuthumi & Ra

#93 **Sunflower**—*Unfolding*
Geometrically Into Your
Glorious Golden Potential Kuthumi, Jerome & Hathors

#94 **Ananas**—*Sprightly Ascension* Kuthumi, Mother Mary
into the Helical Construction & Archangel Nathaniel
of the Fiery Red Group
Alignments of Higher
Vibrational Reality

#95 **Pomegranate**—*Trinitizing* Mother Mary, Thoth
the Self into Spherical Unity & Hiawatha

#96 **Star Fruit**—*Revering the Self* Kuthumi, Mother Mary
as the Divine Image of Infinity & Mary Magdalene

#97 **Papaya**—*Pentagons Create* Kuthumi, Archangel
Dodecahedral Geometries Michael & St. Germain
that allow for Higher
Vibrational Realities of
Orange-Gold Creativity
and Connectivity

#98 **Jackfruit**—*Opening Your* Archangel Gabriel, Mother
Reality Via Axiotonal Lines Mary & Hiawatha
of Ever-present Connection

#99 **Golden- Orange Tomato**— Ra, Kuthumi, Mother Mary
 Finding and Expressing & Mary Magdalene
 Divinity Within, Across
 Simultaneous Time

Appendix 3
Spirit Collaborators—In their Own Words

Spirit Collaborators—In their Own Words

Archangel Gabriel—Beloved brethren, it is with joy and delight that I enfold you in the light of the new dispensation of Source, of being birthed yet again into a new understanding of spirituality, of letting go of the inhibitions to freedom, of claiming your multicolored cloaks of the royal, regal aspects of your divine self. Claim your right to become the masters yet again, those who heroically came to play this game so that Source could experience him/herself via individuation. You are the heroes. You are the gods. And so it is.

Archangel Michael—Beloved Masters, in this time of your rapid reawakening into the light of Source, in this time of reclaiming who you really are, I send you energetics as you read this message, of love, light and the infinite potentials of your true being. You, solar expression of Source are reading this book for a purpose. You are on a path of enlarging yourself into the infinite, fractaling aspects of multidimensionality. Congratulations on where you are in your journey right now. It is perfect. Know that you are guided and loved every step of the way. I am Michael. And so it is.

Archangel Nathaniel—Be bright and star-like, beloved ones, for you, in your ever-present, ever-infinite forms of beingness have always shone out in the forefront of all realities. I have known you as many forms of consciousness in higher realms, where you have interacted with the Elohim energies I derive from, and in each knowing of your vast, higher concepts and expressions of self, I have known your magnificent potentials at this moment of the recalibration of your individuation into higher group formations yet again. Congratulations on this moment in space time. Step into your star selves with ease and with grace, and you will resonate with your higher selves. And so it is.

Archangel Rafael—Greetings, beloved Masters. Your innocence is about to be re-envisioned, redefined and re-enlightened into a wider perspective. Yes, you have always been innocent lambs, but ones with blinders across your eyes, with many filters, engendering the fears, the shame, the hatreds. Let yourself be re-envisioned into the light. I bless you beloved ones. I am Rafael.

Charles Dickens—Hello to you, reader. Well, you might ask, what is a 19th century English novelist doing in a book called "Timeless Awakening"? Well I might ask you to consider that all the famous novelists of the genre have been part of a light family soul agreement to wake up those who were ready, at the time, to the possibilities and potentialities of change, via metaphor, plot and character. And so it is that this channel, Shariq, being of my soul family, resonated with my metaphorical contributions. Please excuse some of the idiomatic use. The verbiage is mine, and all the allusory aspects of allaying the illusions, are my cause and my delight. And so it is.

Goddess Hathor—I have been known in Egyptian times for my fertility, my creativity, my mastery of the understandings of new deliverances and gifts for humanity. It is this seed of fertility that I leave in this book for you. A seed that implants not only the inherent creativity and fertility of your Goddess self, but a seed that also allows you to batten yourself, through the feeding of your own body with the spiritual light that is now enfolding your planet, into a form of bringing forth your own creamy milk of nurturance, creation and divination. Many blessings.

Genoa—I am a being from the 5th Dimension who has served several lifetimes in monasteries, especially in Italy. As I expressed my divinity in an Earthly frame during a time of descension, I often found a way to connect my love for God with my love for my brothers and sisters around me. And this is the message I hope to convey in my contribution to this book. Many blessings.

Hathors—Our group energetic contribution to this magnificent endeavor, our 5th dimensional and higher group sensation and particularation of Goddess weavings of understanding, have allowed Shariq to integrate aspects of the Divine Feminine reawakening that will be an essential part of reclaiming your higher selves in a balanced form. We thank you, brave pioneers, for the steps you are taking to reclaim your birthright as magnificent spiritual beings of divine feminine creativity balanced with divine masculine expression. Let the miracles now unveil themselves in your life. Al-ma-soh-na.

Hiawatha—O-ay-ya-e-am-a. Greetings, blessed child of the new age. I warrior, and reconciliator of the past, bridging the knowledge of the ancient ones to the current timeline, and grounding into your current reality the manifestations of words in this book, as I did in my lifetime in bridging my peoples with the white man, I come to salute your emergence into adulthood, into leaving behind what you were taught by those with limited knowledge, for they were part of a game that included many experiences, including violence, as I found out. But in the frequencies of acceptance, grounding into Nature, and the nature of all things, much can be transmuted and let go. These are the frequencies I lend and re-send to you through Shariq.

Ismael—I am Ismael, greeter and divinator and connector of the Abrahamic religions. I seeded the potential for the continuity and also the reverberation of duality as conflict amongst the Abrahamic religions. I mention this for I have no judgment around this from a higher perspective, as you should not about any event in your life. It has all been part of a game you have been playing. And it is about to reach its finale! Many blessings. I AM That I AM.

Jacob—I have seen much in my time, and I have shared my fruits, that which I only glimpsed, up the ladder of ascension, with humanity. Yet I can only begin to share with you now, O beloved Reader, how many fruits, how many ladders and pathways there are as you proceed: infinite. For it is infinity from whence you came, and it is towards the infinite that you progress now. Go in peace and prosperity. I am Jacob.

Jan—Hay-Ya-O-Wey. I, shaman of Incan times come forward to work the magic of understanding the timelessness of all there is within the moment of communion with the land. It is this land that will guide, you, your planet Gaia, in her work of creative endeavour and ascension. It is she who will show you the next step within your manifested form. Stay true and close to the flowers, the birds and the fruits of her mightiness. Hay-ya-O-way.

Jerome—I am an earlier incarnation of the author, Shariq, within your timeline, a priest and monk from the eighteenth century who was interested in Nature, and collected and examined, the stamens, stems and colors of the creations of the Lord. I was also an incipient scientist and took many notes on the unfolding and leavenings of the light within the miracles of Nature. It is this energy that I have added and continued within Shariq with my energetics. Blessings.

Justinian—I am an ascended being from the 5th dimension, who played many roles in life, disseminating pearls of wisdom, and sometimes, even though I was a leader, I did not connect with the whole, the body of people that I led. And, so, I come forward with my contribution to this book to help enlarge one of the lessons I learnt along the way of my journey that might apply to you: the importance of working with others, and in seeing the larger pattern, the larger design behind all events and situations in life.

Kahlil Gibran—May you, O Reader, be forever evergreen in your new foliage of light. May you, O Reader, be always beloved of yourself, for you are, indeed, the love of all. May you, O Reader claim your right to be the leader of this New Age, as you are, indeed, the spiritual warrior of higher light. In these three sentences I trinitize your potentials into a new unity of glandular rebirthing as your hormonal system realigns over time, to your new manifested light body. And so it is.

Kampala—Greetings to you, O reader. I am a Lemurian energy from Telos, from the caverns of Mt. Shasta, where I made my reacquaintance with Shariq in a reassembly of multidimensional communion into the caverns of light and Christed being. And so it is that just like we have held the light and potential for humanity, waiting for this time of ascension, so it is that you have done your part in playing this game very well, dear brothers and sisters. Find the poetry within your soul, accept who you have been, and assimilate your own God self in the recognition of your original Lemurian light. And so it is.

Kuthumi—Greetings, beloved ones. I am Kuthumi, and I come on the rays of love and wisdom. An ascended master I am. And an ascended master not only are you becoming, but already are, within the simultaneity of time from where my consciousness sits. I observe your growth, your many potentials with fondness and with joy. Claim your mantle of glory, dearest one. You are strong, beloved and full of the Sun-God fire of Source. And so it is. Many blessings.

Lady Guinivere—I am Guinivere of Camelot. I have been known for my beauty. I have been known for my magnificence. I have been known for stirring the pot, so to speak. It is a function of the melding of these attributes that I seed energetically to this delicious modern volume of reawakening. For you are all beautiful; you are all magnificent; and you are all stirring the pot for humanity by choosing to awaken. Blessings, dearest children of the Light.

Lao-Tzu—Well, well. They used to say in ancient times that nothing comes very easy, that it needs to be worked on and meditated upon before the lesson can be learned. I am happy to note, in this time of reawakening and rapid ascension, that this is no longer the case. You can proceed with your ascension rapidly now, O students. I lend my words and energetics to this work to allow for a transformation of the old idioms into the new energetics of permission to become who you came here to be, rapidly now.

Lord Buddha—Stay aligned with your highest potentials, dearest ones. Your light allows you now to rapidly claim nirvana while still embodied on an ascending Earth. This has never been seen before. And so I bless you with the vermilion mark of the Sindhoo, O enlightened one!

Mary Magdalene—Blessings, precious ones. I am Mary Magdalene and I greet you in the presence of divine light, love and beauty. It is your own beauty that many in this magnificent work have referred to again and again, and it is this beauty that I will remark on as well, for this what I see, precious ones, when I observe you reading these words. For you are beautiful beyond compare, for you are of the Christed light. Many blessings.

Merlin—As you stay aligned with your own natural, magical nature, so it is that the Nature of your own awakening, within the realms of this book, will allow you to claim the mastery that is the alchemical change and affirmation of the self into what it has always been: ascended, magnificent, beautiful. Claim your mastery, beautiful one, and let the magic of life unveil itself to you. Many blessings. I am Merlin.

Mother Mary—I am Mother Mary and I come forward to greet you in divine light, love, truth and wisdom. Know, beloved ones, that a new day is dawning now, that a new age is coming to the forefront rapidly, as the thunderstorms of change provide the cleansing waters, the baptisms into a new time of being light, and of being the loving essence of source. Claim your birthright to be free by seeing the thunderstorms of change as an opportunity to outpace your previous hopes into the magnificent realms of unbounded destiny. Stay in Peace. I am Mother Mary.

Micana—I am a divine feminine essence of 10th dimensional eternity that has come forward to assist in divining and contouring the emotional resonances of color, smell and taste that can be used to create anew within the simultaneous time of all there is. I urge you, beloved ones, to believe that in the creative soup of all there is, it is a higher aspect of you that has always created your reality. May the divine creative feminine self be birthed in you anew to create the balanced Creator-God you have always been. Many blessings.

Najimi—I am an elemental being that works with the larger devas of the Daffodils. I bring forward my perspective of the honeyed, sentient nature of simply working within and exhibiting the true inner nature of the golden smells of daffodils.

Ra—Who or what is Ra, you might ask. Yes, Ra is a Sun-god energy from Egyptian times. Yes, Ra is a form of group consciousness that has parlayed messages of note to humanity again and again across your manifested history. And, yes, Ra is part of a cosmic council that oversees your particular Galaxy. We are vast, we are infinite. And so are you. Mahalo, Inhala.

Rembrandt—Well, it is with the glory and understanding, with the precision and eye of a master painter that you will find yourself rebirthed as this ascension continues apace. Stay aligned with the knowledge that, as you claim your birthright to claim the knowledge of Source, you can be as masterful, creative, expressive and precise as I. In this your truth will be revealed. Many blessings. I am Rembrandt.

Robert Burns—Well, me laddies, you are about to burn yourself into a new fire of light, the light that is perfect, the essence of your God-selves. In the beauty of the red rose comes the emblem of what has always been true, even when I was incarnated amongst the warfare in Scotland: no highlander can ever claim the high ground without first acknowledging his love for all. And so it is. Many blessings.

Shakespeare—We are a group consciousness from various realities that chose to embody in several individuals during the late 16th and early 17th centuries in Britain to bring forward works for humanity to marvel at, and play with, as mirrors of the many games they have been acting out as humans, since the fall of consciousness. The individuals, whose identities we will not reveal at this point, worked together to co-author the plays. The historical personage known as Shakespeare was a part of this plan, and contributed, but only as part of the larger group effort to manifest these works for humanity. And so it is. Many blessings.

St. Germain—I have been a scribe of the Masters, like this channel Shariq, and I have shown the beauty of Source, as this one does. Yet I knew always that the alchemy of reawakening would work its own magic, its own alchemy of refined possibilities. The possibilities for positioning yourself for the 5th, 6th, 7th dimension or even higher is within your grasp right now, beloved Masters. I did not imagine that the opportunities, the possibilities would be so expansive. Yet, so it is. And as a continuing scribe for Source, within the unity of all there is, like this channel, let me affirm that the time is NOW to claim your mastery. May the violet light always be with you. Blessings.

Thoth—Greetings, O Human awakeners into this time of Emerald reawakening. From the multidimensional Halls of Amenti I greet you and partake my energies of this volume to let you know, in no uncertain terms, that you are vast, magnificent, and are here, as part of the family of the light to reawaken into your vast light, and I am overseeing this process for you, as I have done for eons of time. Many blessings.

Glossary

Akashic Records—Akasha is a Sanskrit word meaning "sky" or "ether". The term Akashic Records is used to refer to information from Source that was encoded in non-linear time envelopes of light that are accessible via clairvoyance through those who have the eyes to see, those who are awakened. The records, in the infinite wisdom of all there is, include all histories across all timelines of the Planet Earth, of humanity, and of the **Fall of Consciousness**.

And So Be It—An affirmation, a statement of the Creaor-God self embodied in human form, claiming the right to create from the Akash, the source particles whatever he/she chooses to, claiming the right to consciously align with his/her **God/Goddess** self and divine destiny.

Buddha, Bodhisattva—Siddharta Gautama was a spiritual teacher from ancient India, who founded the philosophy and spiritual truths of Buddhism, a loving religion focused on the truth of reincarnation and of letting the illusions of life be released to see the reality of love and light, that is the basis of nirvana, or freedom from the matrix and karmic wheel. Ahead of his times, and a harbinger of the Spiritual New Age awakening, Buddha, meaning "the awakened one" is indeed an appropriate title for his teachings, and, as we each continue our waking up journey now, with the Shift in Consciousness, we, too become awakened, to our highest potentials, or Bodhisattvas.

Christ Consciousness—The knowledge and fundamental creative force of unified love and wholeness, allowing for all creation to express and be without judgment, witnessing with love and light the beauty of Source experiencing him/her self. This form of consciousness begins to be accessible in the 5th dimension and beyond.

Christed Self, Being—The aspect of Self that is ascended, that lives in close communion with the Source of light and love in the higher planes.

Creator Gods—Beings of light charged with creating manifested realms, allowing for the creation of the infinity of all there is to be expressed, within the light envelopes of the original codings of love, which are released and desired to be experienced by Source.

Ego—The aspect of the human consciousness that was activated with the Fall of Consciousness into the 3rd dimension of duality. Also known as the "rational mind", this is the aspect of self that tries to linearize and put logical construction around that which is divine, infinite, non-linear and epistemologically unreachable via the brain. Aspects of the ego also work to create, within the dualistic framework of the 3rd dimension, judgments about good and bad, right and wrong, and sets of belief systems about how to proceed in life, and how to measure success, among many other functions.

Elohim—The Elohim are a set of frequency light vibrational consciousness that are truly aligned with the unity emanation from which all proceeds, from which all subdivides, that is Source. And so, the Elohim, in their infinite access to the all there is, of the Universal Mind and Wisdom of Source, manage and monitor the light, heat and sound envelopes that provide the parameters and templates for the creation of both physical and non-physical universes, galaxies and stars. In their infinite wisdom, the Elohim, whose light is now beginning to be made available to awakening humanity, enfold and encode new aspects of Creation, including the co-Creation of the New Earth with humanity and the many beings of light that are working with them.

The "Fall"—At the time of the Fall of Atlantis, in this free will zone of Earth, the energetics of those not aligned with the light of Source, allowed for distortions to become manifested in a very dramatic way on Earth, allowing for several timelines to intersect, crash and compress with each other, forcing not only the Earth to be dissected into a much compressed, dense version of reality, that has been our world of duality, but also reconfigured humanity's bodily systems into less active chakras, a greater separation from Source, and introduced lower vibrational frequencies such as fear, anger, hatred, revenge, punishment, greed, that could not have existed in the higher frequencies, before the Fall. The current Shift in Consciousness, with the galactic alignments that have been discussed in the introduction, allows, for not only a resurrection of light and love into pre-"Fall" Atlantean times, but much more to be rebirthed and co-created by awakening humanity at this time of planetary, galactic and universal ascension.

Fibonnaci Sequence—In Mathematics, the Fibonnaci numbers are the numbers in the following integer sequence: 0, 1, 1, 2, 3, 5, 8, 13, 21, 34, 55, 89, 144…and so on, where each number is the sum of the two numbers prior to it. In this sequence of adding and building with love on what has been before, we create the beauty of life and Nature.

First Ray of Light—We refer here to the First Ray of Creation, which represents the Divine Will of the Creator, and the infinite wisdom and love that represents this Will, from which all Creation proceeds. Within our manifested Universe, the First Ray of Creation has been foremost in its amplification of new geometric codes that have allowed for the experience of density, free will, and the aspects of separation that have allowed All There Is to experience itself.

Golden Mean—In Mathematics, the golden mean, or golden ratio is said to occur when the ratio of the sum of the quantities (a + b) to the larger quantity (a) is equal to the ratio of the larger quantity (a) to the smaller one (b). This ratio is an irrational constant: 1.6180339...This constant occurs naturally in the Fibonnnaci Sequence, in an approximation, as the ratio of a number to the number immediately preceding it in the Sequence. It is thus a part of the Nature of Creation, that as the ratios of the Fibonnaci Sequence are the process of unfolding, it is this Golden Ratio, or Golden Mean that is the Midas touch of Source from which all is manifested, from universes, to the atoms and subatomic particles that make up your bodies.

Great Central Sun—The magnificence of Source holographed into a Solar Disc that is infinite, holographic and multidimensional. This portal between dimensional frontiers allows for a light-filled set of encodements and sound envelopes to be seeded in new realms, assuring for the conformity of all Creation to the larger encodements of Creation by Source within the light and love of all things.

God/Goddess—The energetics and formulation of Source into the Creator energies of manifestation who are the prime movers of the creation of universes and galaxies including our Milky Way Galaxy. We are currently in the process, via the ascension, of merging the still point of our own God/Goddess self, located within the sacred chamber of our Heart chakra, and merging it with the God/Goddess light of our Milky Way Galaxy, our Universe, and beyond.

Guides—Each incarnated human enters this game of 3rd dimensional duality with 3 primary guides who have been whispering in our ears since the time we were babies. These guides, who are generally from your soul family, often have played in this game themselves, so they know how to assist you in very tangible and practical ways. As the Shift in Consciousness proceeds and we start waking up more and more, we start to get additional guides, even Ascended Master guides who provide additional frequencies of information, knowledge, and encouragement. Our original guides always stay with us; yet we continue to attract more and more loving attention and guidance from many beings of light, as we continue to move through the veils of limitation that have been our experience.

Higher Self—The Higher Self is that aspect of Self that is not only multidimensionally aware and has played the process of unfolding the separation of the spark of source that it is, but represents also, in its many aspects and representations of you, the rungs of the infinite ladder back to the heart of Source, the love from which you come. Just like Jacob's ladder took him to see God, so it is the rungs of ascension, up the rungs of the consciousnesses that make up your multidimensional selves, imbued with Christ Consciousness, allow you to traverse up, through the Shift of Consciousness, to know yourself, for ultimately your Highest Self is Source, combined in a monadic unity with all things, from which all springs.

I AM That I AM—An affirmation and statement, encoded in light-heat formations and references to the original signature and sound of the origin of all there is, affirming the multidimensional nature of our consciousness, aligning and divining in a unity with the God-head, or Source.

Karma—Within traditional Hindu and Buddhist traditions, karma is known to be the law of cause and effect, of the need for a balancing of all actions to bring them back into equilibrium. Within the energetics of the 3rd dimensional game we have all been playing, this has meant that energy that had emotional charge around it, in a lifetime, became stuck in our **PEMS body** as magnetic attractors, bringing to us events in subsequent moments across our lifetimes where we would be afforded opportunities to bring this karma to our consciousness, and release it.

Kundalini—Kundalini is a Sanskrit word that means "coiled". There are many meanings that this term has spiritually, and in the larger ascension that we are currently experiencing. In traditional Hindu scriptures the notion has existed of a vast connection to the Source of light via a serpentine energy, that, once opened, allows for a rapid expansion and merge with cosmic insight. This energy is very powerful, and used to take much yogic discipline and instruction to work with carefully, to make sure the body would not be overwhelmed. Now, as the Shift is accelerating, our bodies' frequency is automatically being upgraded, allowing for this cosmic coiling of light within us, to unfurl quite naturally from our lower chakras, connecting us with the creative energies that allow us to express our Creator-God selves. The Kundalini light of Gaia, is also uncoiling at this time, allowing in her awakening, a deeper receiving, and unfurling of the Divine Feminine, creative light, which this energy of expansion and joy, represents.

Law of Fair Exchange—The Law of Fair Exchange, a cosmic law of deep resonance across your manifested Universe, necessitates that all energy be balanced across simultaneous time, so that there is no pushing or pulling in the energy streams of flow. This has manifested in your 3D Earth plane as the law of Karma within the linear envelope of reincarnation that has been your reality. As the Shift proceeds, the Law of Fair Exchange will be available to work with in its higher frequencies, requiring humans, as they ascend, to remember to stay in the vibrations of kindness, integrity and truth. In this, all will flow with balance.

Merkaba—A Merkaba is a geometric alignment and configuration that acts, among its many functions as both a container for the energy and flow that is your multidimensional self, and as an antenna to connect with and resonate with other parts of you that exist in other realms, to bring in and step down information that can assist you in your experience, in the moment. And so it is that the original merkabas of the Octahedron and the Star Tetrahedron, once re-ignited within your auric fields, and spun into higher frequencies of light, will allow you to grow into that resonance and understanding of your multidimensional self. And the unique blueprint of you as a Soul, which you have jumpstarted in recognizing and rebuilding into your conscious awareness by reading this book, will indeed be manifested as your unique, beautiful, colorful geometry, of light, color, and sound as the Shift of Consciousness proceeds.

PEMS Body—This acronym refers to the **P**hysical, **E**motional, **M**ental and **S**piritual bodies, that were split apart at the time of the **Fall of Consciousness**. There is an opportunity now, as the Shift proceeds, to merge these bodies in a unified whole, magnificently recreating the original blueprints and templates of the design of the Adam Kadmon body, allowing for the flow of divine light to be effortless, continuous and a natural state of being in our constant union and communion with the Source of all there is.

Samsara—A Sanskrit word meaning "continuous flow", and which refers to the constant cycle of birth and rebirth that has been the soul's journey of evolution within the apparent linear matrix of 3rd dimensional Earth, post the **Fall in Consciousness**. This word has had connotations of difficulty within the human experience, as in Buddhist traditions, for it has been assumed that it is hard to break out of this cycle and reach freedom, or what the Buddhists call "nirvana". This is changing already with the ongoing Shift in Consciousness.

Endnotes

1   All bolded items are explained in greater detail in the Glossary.

2   Spirit is referring here to "An Ascension Hanbook" by Tony Stubbs (1991)

3   John Keats: "Ode To Autumn."

4   The character Dorothy is referenced from the book The Wizard of Oz by L. Frank Baum.

5   In Latin "mel" means honey.

6   Spirit uses the reference to Napoleon here to emphasize his certainty in fighting for the authentic values of liberty, equality, and fraternity, which helped spread these revolutionary ideas all across Europe, resulting in the Napoleonic civil code, even though he eventually succumbed to destructive energies, and seized power as Emperor.

7   Reference to Olivia-Newton John's song: "Magic".

8   Daphne, in the Greek myth memorialized by Ovid in Metamorphoses, is a symbol of transformation, as she transformed into the flowering of a laurel, reflecting her inner beauty.

9 The Spanish word, Encalado, refers to calcamine, which is used as a whitewash. As the interregnum of the 3rd dimensional consciousness winds down with the Shift, a white washing with the divine white light of a new Spiritual alignment becomes available to all, leading to the freedom to follow your divine destiny with certainty.

10 Sakura is a famed Cherry Blossom tree in Japan, known and celebrated in Japanese culture since ancient times.

11 Spirit uses the word "burnish" here in the Middle English etymology of "browning". Current English usage of the word indicates a sense of brightness, of polish, and this sense is used towards the end of this piece. In a sense, we are always the same, and how we perceive our color, whether we believe in ourselves or not, determines our experience. And, so, the two usages of the word "burnish" in this piece suggests that being bright comes from the inner divine insight and belief that you have always been and always will be a bright manifestation of love and light.

12 The bark of the willow tree contains salicin, which is a chemical similar to aspirin, and has been used for pain relief and anti-inflammatory purposes since ancient times.

13 The Persian word beed-e-majnun refers to the weeping willow, the word majnun, itself, meaning mad, often madly in love.

14 By using the word "ephemeral", Spirit is building the notion of the NOW moment as simultaneous, where nothing exists except that very ephemeral moment, yet all is always available, in the infinity of all there is.

15 Spirit uses the word "thistle" here in primary reference to a pale purple color. Primroses appear in many colors, and the thistle color reflects the incipient stages towards full regal, deep purple spiritual mastery. In Spirit's infinite wisdom, it is interesting to note that, in the other sense of the word, the thistle flower is known for the prickly leaves surrounding it, suggesting both that the process can appear thorny at times, and the awakening process can be like a prick in the finger, alerting and reviving expanded consciousness through the colors and smells of emerging flowerings of consciousness.

16 Archangel Rafael on the placement of this piece: "We would like humanity to embrace eternity, and as they embark in the NOW moment of their incipient Spiritual awakening, to realize that time is infinite and always present. And, hence, there is no need to rush. All will come your way as it is meant to. So do not be afraid that you will run out of time. Do not be afraid of death. As you embrace this eternal truth, your heart chakra embraces the divine, unconditional love it is even more deeply."

17 Hindu god of success.

18 "Puja" is a Sanskrit word meaning reverence. It is also a religious ritual performed by Hindus as an offering to various deities or distinguished persons.

19 Indian name for monarch, derived from the Sanskrit word "rajan"; the consonant "jan" refers to the heart; "ra", of course, can be seen as a reference to the solar sun-god, RA, a co-author of this book.

20   Rhododendron is a genus of flowering plants with over 1,000 species and many different colors.

21   Wordsworth's poem "Daffodils" begins: "I wander'd lonely as a cloud/ That floats on high o'er vales and hills,/ When all at once I saw a crowd,/ A host, of golden daffodils."

22   See Plato's "Phaedrus" and "Republic" for a detailed exposition on his notion of formless archetypes.

23   "Are not two sparrows sold for a penny? Yet not one of them will fall to the ground apart from the will of your Father." Matthew 10:29.

24   "There is a special providence in the fall of a sparrow." Hamlet, Act V, Scene 2, Shakespeare.

25   Here Spirit refers to the ability to practice discernment regarding others' representation of the truth.

26   In Greek mythology, Leda, wife of the King of Sparta, was seduced by Zeus who came to her in the guise of a swan. Her offspring, the twin mortal-immortal gods Castor and Pollux came to symbolize the duality of mortal and immortal existence.

27   In Greek mythology Argos was a giant with 100 eyes. The goddess Hera slew Argos and placed his all-seeing eyes on her sacred bird, the peacock.

28   All bramble fruits, including raspberries and blackberries are aggregate fruits, which mean they are formed by the aggregation of several smaller fruits, called drupelets.

The drupelets are all attached to a structure called the receptacle, which is the fibrous central core of the fruit.

29   "Salaam" is the Arabic word for peace. "As-Salaam" is one of the 99 words of God in the Quran.

30   Harappa is an archeological site in Pakistan where one of the ancient cities of the Indus Valley Civilization reached its apotheosis, around 2,500 BC. Its reddish clay can be observed even in the present day.

31   Spirit uses the word "evangelical" here in its original usage, where it referred to good news, or tidings.

32   "Lessons to trust are gathered from the Lily" Matthew 6:28-30.

33   For centuries, artists have pictured the Angel Gabriel coming to the virgin Mother Mary, with lilies in his hand, to announce that she is to be the mother of Christ.

34   A Star of David pattern, with its interlocking triangles can be seen as a two-dimensional version of a 3D star tetrahedron geometric shape which can be viewed as two interlocking tetrahedrons.

35   Spirit refers here to an etheric grid that channels light frequencies and instructions for the Shift to Gaia, using its specific geometric construction. The geometry of this grid is discussed in detail in Chapter 10, in the piece "Papaya".

36   Spirit is referring here to morning dew drops.

37   The Egyptian blue water lily (N. caerulea), opens its flowers in the morning and then sinks beneath the water at dusk. The ancient Egyptians linked the flower with the rising and the setting of the sun, and thus to the Sun-God, Ra.

38   In botany, phyllotaxis is the pattern of arrangement on the leaves of a stem plant as it spirals up in its growth. A repeating spiral can be represented by a fraction describing the angle of windings per leaf. The numerator and denominator of this fraction normally consists of a Fibonnaci number and its second successor (Wikipedia).

39   In mathematics, the Fibonnaci numbers are the numbers in the following sequence: 0, 1, 1, 2, 3, 5, 8, 13, 21, 34, 55, 89, 144…By definition, the first two Fibonnaci numbers are 0 and 1, and each subsequent number is the sum of the previous two.

40   The golden ratio, also called the golden mean, equal to 1.61803…, is the limit of the ratios of successive terms of the Fibonnaci sequence.

41   The name dandelion originates from the French dent-de-lion, meaning lion's tooth.

42   During the seed dispersal process for the dandelion the flower heads mature into spherical "parachutes" made up of fine hairs, which enable wind-enabled dispersal over wide distances . (Wikipedia)

43   A geodesic dome is a spherical or partial-spherical lattice shell based on network of great circles (geodesics) lying on the surface of a sphere. (Wikipedia)

44   The 5-pointed star, or pentagram, is formed by the 5 in-
      tersecting diagonals of a pentagon.

45   Leonardo da Vinci's drawing of the Vitruvian Man (c.
      1485) depicts the 5 extremities branching out of man's
      torso: 2 arms, 2 legs and the head. If lines are drawn con-
      necting the points where each extremity bisects the
      sphere surrounding the man, a pentagram, or 5-point
      star is formed.

46   The ancient Greeks discovered that the human body is
      structured according to the golden mean, or phi ratio.
      This ratio stays approximately constant at 1.618 whether
      in measuring distances of two bones of a finger of one
      hand, or in the distance between the nose and the base
      of the neck, the distance between the forearm and the
      wrist, and so on. (Michael S.Schneider—"A Beginner's
      Guide to Constructing the Universe—Mathematical Ar-
      chetypes of Nature, Art, and Science").

47   Axiotonal lines were first discussed in "The Book of
      Knowledge: The Keys of Enoch" by J.J.Hurtak (1973), and
      refer to the reconnective fabric between the grid lines in
      our bodies and grid lines in our Universe, which, in their
      reconnection to each other via axiatonal lines of renew-
      al, allow humanity at the time of the Shift to reconnect
      with their ever-present higher aspects of self, bringing
      in quantum knowledge and consciousness within their
      grasp as the merge with all there is proceeds apace.

Made in the USA
Charleston, SC
11 March 2011